RESERVED CASES

ACCORDING TO

THE CODE OF CANON LAW

A DISSERTATION

Submitted to the Faculty of Canon Law of the Catholic University of America in partial fulfilment of the requirements for the Degree of Doctor of Canon Law

BY THE
REV. EDWARD VINCENT DARGIN,
S. T. B., J. C. L.
Of the Archdiocese of New York

WASHINGTON, D. C.
1924

Nihil Obstat:

THOMAS J. SHAHAN,

Censor Deputatus.

Washingtonii, D. C., die 26 Maii, 1924.

Imprimatur:

MICHAEL J. CURLEY,

Archiepiscopus Baltimorensis.

Baltimorae, die 26 Maii, 1924.

TABLE OF CONTENTS

Reserved Cases According to the Code of Canon Law

INTRODUCTION

The object of this dissertation is to examine the canons on reserved cases in the Code of Canon Law, and, with the aid of the new legislation, to discuss the principal problems directly or indirectly connected with the subject of reserved cases.

It is scarcely necessary to call attention to the practical importance of this subject. Very often the liceity, and some times even the validity of a confessor's absolution are affected by the law of the Church on reserved cases. Consequently, to exercise his office properly, the confessor must know the doctrine of the Church on reserved sins; he must know what they are, what effect they produce, what faculties he possesses to absolve from them, what effect the ignorance of the penitent may have upon them and the various other connected questions he may be called upon to solve in the confessional. To be ignorant of these would be to run the risk of doing grave injustice to the penitent, seriously violating the law of the Church, and failing in the divine duty of judging when he is to bind and when he is to loose.

Until a comparatively few years ago there was scarcely any section of canon law or moral theology more confused or more involved than that dealing with reserved cases, complicated, as it was, by the contradictory opinions of canonists and theologians. Practically every phase of the subject gave rise to disputes and disagreements, so much so that the theological student was sometimes tempted to consider it too hopeless a tangle to unravel. But the Code presents a new statement of the legislation on reserved cases, a statement which is, on the whole, clear and intelligible. Though it can not be claimed that the text, of itself, solves all the points formerly disputed, it does explicitly solve some, and implicitly indicates a solution to others.

The first section of this dissertation will be devoted to an explanation of reservation in general. Then, in keeping with the fundamental distinction between a sin reserved *ratione sui* and a sin reserved *ratione censurae*, the remainder of the work will be divided into two principal parts, the first treating of sins reserved *ratione sui* and the second of sins reserved *ratione censurae.*

I. RESERVATION IN GENERAL

1. *Definition*

The object of a code of law is to establish laws and consequently it does not properly come within its scope to set forth definitions. Yet, for clarity sake, the Code often describes, rather than defines, various canonical terms. Canon 893 furnishes an example of this and from its wording it is evident that the Legislator here describes what a reserved case is.

Qui ordinario iure possunt audiendi confessiones potestatem concedere aut ferre censuras, possunt quoque, excepto Vicario Capitulari et Vicario Generali sine mandato speciali, nonnullos casus ad suum avocare iudicium, inferioribus absolvendi potestatem limitantes.

Haec avocatio dicitur "reservatio casuum."

In accordance with the description given in this canon, a reserved case may be defined as: Avocatio quorundum peccatorum et censurarum ad superioris iudicium a legitimo superiore facta, inferiorbus absolvendi potestatem limitando—reservation is the summoning of certain sins and censures to the judgment of a superior tribunal, by a legitimate superior, whereby the power of inferiors to absolve is limited.

When a legitimate superior grants jurisdiction he may, if he wishes, grant it in a limited degree. Since he is free to grant it or not, he is a fortiori able to grant it in a limited way. He may, for example, limit its exercise to a certain class of people by merely granting jurisdiction to hear children's confessions; or he may restrict its exercise to certain places as, for example, the limits of some parish; or he may restrict it to a defined time by granting jurisdiction only for three months or a year; or, finally a superior may limit the power of absolving in confessors, who derive their jurisdiction from him or whose tribunals are inferior to his, by restricting their jurisdiction in such a way that they can not absolve from certain sins, and censures. It is this latter restriction or limitation of jurisdiction that constitutes what is known as "Reservation."

The direct effect of reservation is to bring some cases to the tribunal of a superior for judgment or absolution; the means used to bring about this effect is the limitation or restriction of the power to absolve in inferiors. Reservation, therefore, directly affects the confessor by limiting his power; it affects the penitent or delinquent only indirectly inasmuch as he presents himself to the confessor who is directly affected. In other words, the delinquent's inability to be absolved is a consequence of the confessor's limited jurisdiction; the confessor's limited jurisdiction is not a consequence of the delinquent's inability to be absolved.

2. *Division*

Just as sins and censures are removed by absolution, so too the restriction of power to absolve, or reservation, may concern either sins or censures. In a reserved case, a sin may have a censure attached to it or it may not. If it has not, it is then clear that the reservation directly affects the sin, that is the jurisdiction that has been directly restricted by the superior is the jurisdiction to absolve from the sin in question. But if a censure is attached to some sin, there are then three possibilities —the superior may directly reserve the power to absolve from the sin, or he may directly reserve the power to absolve from the censure, or he may directly reserve the power to absolve from both the sin and the censure. [1] In the first hypothesis, namely when a sin has not a censure attached to it, and the superior reserves the power to absolve from the sin, the latter is then said to be reserved *ratione sui.* In the second hypothesis, namely when a sin has a censure attached to it, and the superior directly reserves the power to absolve from this censure, a natural consequence is that the sin is also indirectly

[1] Vermeersch—Creusen, II, No. 175.

reserved if the censure is one which impedes the use of the sacraments, because, by the very nature of the case, the sin cannot be absolved until the censure is removed. In this second hypothesis, the power to absolve from the censure is *directly* reserved, the power to absolve from the sin is *indirectly* reserved and consequently the sin is said to be reserved *ratione censurae,* in contradistinction to a sin reserved directly *ratione sui.* When power to absolve from a sin is only indirectly reserved, that is when the sin is reserved *ratione censurae,* if one is excused from incurring the censure, or if the censure is removed by absolution, the sin is no longer reserved and any confessor can absolve from it. But when the power to absolve from a sin has been directly reserved, that is when a sin is reserved *ratione sui,* it remains reserved even though a censure attached to it is not incurred or is absolved. And so in the third hypothesis, mentioned above, namely when the superior directly reserved both the power to absolve from the sin and from the censure, the sin is reserved in a twofold manner, *ratione sui* and *ratione censurae* and even though the latter reservation should not be incurred because the censure was not, the sin would nevertheless remain reserved *ratione sui.*

The generic term *reserved case* is used to designate any or all of the above mentioned hypotheses, that is a *reserved case* may designate a reserved sin or a reserved censure or both simultaneously. Consequently, the terms *reserved sin* and *reserved censure* are subdivisions or species of the general term *reserved case.* Thus, for example, § 1 and § 2, of canon 893 apply to reserved sins and reserved censures and so the term *reservatio casuum* is used; but § 3 of this canon states: "quod attinet *ad reservatio censurarum,* servetur praescriptum can. 2246, 2247."

There is, therefore, a fundamental distinction between a reserved sin and a reserved censure. Most of the confusion resulting from commentator's expositions of the doctrine on reserved cases has been caused by their failure to clearly indicate the distinction between reserved sins and reserved censures, and the consequent application of the norms governing the reservation of sins *ratione censurae* to the reservation of sins reserved *ratione sui.* From § 3 of canon 893 it is now clear, beyond any question of doubt, that the distinction between a reserved sin and a reserved censure must be insisted upon, and the fact that the Code treats the legislation concerning reserved censures in a distinct and separate section from that in which it places the legislation concerning reserved sins shows that there are distinct norms governing each, and that a single set of norms can not be applied promiscuously to both.

The canons which immediately follow canon 893 refer, generally, only to reserved sins, or, as one author expresses it: "In capite autem 'De Poenitentia' Codex fere non agit nisi de reservatis peccatis." [2] They only refer to reserved censures when the latter are expressly mentioned, or are included by the very nature of the case. The general norms governing reserved censures and sins reserved *ratione censurae* are to be sought in canons 2246-2254 and not in canons 893-900, except for a few which are passingly referred to in the latter section. In keeping with this fundamental distinction, the body of this dissertation is divided into two sections, one on sins reserved *ratione sui,* the other on reserved censures and sins reserved *ratione censurae,* and this division will be observed as closely as possible, even to the extent of repeating some matter in the second section rather than group both sections together when common points are referred to.

3. *Historical Origin*

Although the Pope and Bishops always possessed the right to reserve cases, they did not begin to exercise this right until a comparatively late date. No trace of reservation can be found in the earliest centuries and Hinschius declares that there is no foundation for the assertion that reservation existed as

[2] Vermeersch—Creusen, II, No. 175.

early as the fifth century.[3] Since most of the authors[4] who discuss the history of reservation do not place its origin earlier than the ninth century and since it is certain that the practice had reached its highest point of development at the time of the Council of Trent, it appears that the origin, growth and development of the use of the power to reserve took place from the ninth century to the time of the Council of Trent.

The most satisfactory explanation of the origin of episcopal reservations is that they are an outgrowth of the ancient system of public penance. According to this system, whether confession was made publicly or privately, the penance assigned had to be performed publicly and the reconciliation which came at the close of the period of public penance was a ceremony of marked publicity and solemnity. This solemn, public ceremony of reconciliation could be performed as a rule only by the bishop. Over the whole area of Western Europe with the exception of the British Isles, penance was public, reconciliation was public and the minister of reconciliation was the bishop; wheresoever the records have come down to us the procedure of the central church on the Coena Domini shows the bishops reconciling public penitents in a function of imposing solemnity.[5] About the ninth century, however, a distinction arose between the penance inflicted for public offences and the penance inflicted for private offences, and Watkins declares that it became a commonplace of Christian practice that public offences call for public penance and that private offences are sufficiently met by private penance.[6]

This practice of public penance for public offences and private penance for private offences represents the first step towards Episcopal reservations; since only the bishop could grant reconciliation to public penitents, these cases came to be

---

[3] Hinschius, IV, 102, note 2.

[4] Thomassin, Pars I, Lib. II, cap. XIII; Van Espen, pars II, tit. VI, cap. VII; Benedict XIV, *De Synoda Dioecesana,* lib. V, cap. 4; Hinschius, IV, 102; Le Canoniste Contemporain, XLIII, 115.

[5] Watkins, II, 751.

[6] Ibidem, II, 696.

considered as reserved to the bishop. Van Espen states :[7] "Cum vero de gravioribus quibuslibet peccatis multis saeculis poenitentia *publica* acta fuerit etiam graviorum criminum absolutio *Episcopis* reservata censebatur. Dum autem sensim poenitentia *publica* pro occultis desiit, etiam occultorum criminum absolutio Presbyteris concredita fuit; publicorum vero, pro quibus publica poenitentia erat peragenda, absolutio Episcopis longo tempore reservata fuit; ut proinde reservatio quorumdam criminum, sive casuum hodie ab Episcopis fieri solita, nonnisi exigua sit pristinae auctortatis Episcopalis particula." Thomassin also accounts for the origin of Episcopal reservation as a development of the ancient system of public penance. [8]

In the year 933, Bishop Ruthenis of Verona stated in a letter to his priests; "De occultis peccatis poenitentiam vos dare posse scitote: de publicis ad nos deferendum agnoscite."[9] A similar declaration was made by the Synod of Limoges, held in the year 1031: "Presbyteri de ignotis causis, episcopi de notis excommunicare est, ne episcopi vilescas potestas."[10]

During the 12th century the practice of reserving cases gradually spread and extended to occult as well as public crimes. Thus the Council of London, held in the year 1102 reserved unnatural crimes to the Bishop, [11] the Council of York ordered perjurers to be sent to the bishop for absolution [12] and Eudes bishop of Paris declared: "Sacerdotes majora reservent majoribus, in confessionibus, sicut homicidia sacrilegia, peccata contra naturam, incestus, et stupra virginum, injectiones manuum in parentes, vota facta et huismodi etc." [13]

The growth of the practice of reservation is indicated by the long list of reserved cases established by the Council of Arles in 1275, Cologne in 1280 and Mines in 1284. [14]

[7] Pars. II, tit. VI, No. VI
[8] Pars. I, lib. II, cap. XIV, No. 2.
[9] M P L, CXXXVI, 567.
[10] Mansi, 19, 537.
[11] Hardouin, VI, 1866.
[12] Ibidem, VI, 1932.
[13] Ibidem, VI, 1940.
[14] Ibidem, VII, 729, 829, 913.

Papal reservations most probably originated from the custom of sending cases to Rome for absolution.[15] It appears certain that the power of bishops was in no way restricted by Papal reservations until the eleventh century. From the fact that the Council of Limoges[16] prohibited priests to send penitents to Rome for absolution without the permission of the bishops, Van Espen argues that the bishops possessed unrestricted power to absolve: "Hinc consequens est Episcopos nequaquam credisse, etiam gravissimorum criminum poenitentiam imponendam aut eorum absolutionem Romanis Pontificibus reservatam, quandoquidem nemini suorum Parochianorum pro quocumque crimine permitterent inconsulto Episcopo ad Romanum Pontificem habere recursum."[17]

The practice of sending penitents to Rome for absolution began about the ninth century.[18] The Council of Limoges ordered that those guilty of homicide would have to go to Rome for absolution. The case most frequently sent to Rome by bishops was the crime of striking clerics. By the eleventh century the practice of penitents going to Rome for absolution at the command of their own bishops was very common. It was only natural that a law of papal reservation would result and the fact that the first definite example of a papal reservation concerns the case most frequently referred to Rome by the bishops themselves gives weight to the opinion that papal reservations originated in this manner.

The earliest definite, general legislation establishing a papal reserved case appears to be the famous chapter "Si quis suadente diabolo" of the Second Lateran Council held in the year 1139.[19] From this time reservation to the Holy See became more and more frequent but these were all cases of reserved

[15] Thomassin, pars. I, lib. II, cap. XIII; Van Espen, pars. II, tit. VI, cap. VIII; Le Canoniste Contemporain, XLIII, 115.

[16] Mansi, 19, 537.

[17] Pars II, tit. VI, cap. VIII.

[18] Benedict XIV, *De Synodo Dioecesana,* V, 4.

[19] II Lateran Council, can, 15.

censures. The first case reserved because of the sin is probably that established by Sixtus V against those who simoniacally promoted to orders[20] but this was later abrogated by Clement VIII.[21] The next reservation of sin *ratione sui* was established by Benedict XIV against those who falsely accused a confessor of the crime of solicitation, and this has continued down to the present time.[22]

4. *The Purpose of Reservation*

In order to properly understand the concept and nature of reservation it is most important to ascertain the purpose of reservation.[23] It has been pointed out that reservation is a restriction of the power to absolve imposed by a competent superior on inferior tribunals. What is the purpose of this restriction, why does the superior limit the power to absolve in certain cases? Is the primary object of reservation, of sin or of censure, to punish the guilty penitent by making it more difficult for him to obtain absolution when he has committed a very serious sin or crime? Or is the primary purpose of reservation disciplinary rather than penal, i.e., is it not a means of bringing more serious cases before those who, by reason of official position, learning and experience, are best qualified to handle the case in the best interests of ecclesiastical discipline and to supply the proper remedies for some evil which threatens to overthrow ecclesiastical discipline?

The Code does not give a direct answer to these questions, yet it furnishes ample evidence that the primary purpose of reservation is not to punish the delinquent but to bring more serious cases before those best qualified to give them the judgment and prudent consideration they require.

[20] Sixtus V, *Sanctum et salutare,* 5 Jan. 1589; Cod. Iur. Can. Fontes, I, 166.
[21] Clement VIII, Const. *Romanum Pontificem,* 28 Feb. 1596, par. 2; Cod. Iur. Can. Fontes, I, 182.
[22] Benedict XIV, Const. *Sacramentum Poenitentiæ,* 1 June 1741, Doc. V in the Code; Canon 894.
[23] Irish Ecclesiastical Record, XVIII, 627.

A negative argument that reservation is not a penalty can be drawn from the fact that reservation is not listed among the canonical penalties. Moreover in the description of reservation given in canon 893, there is no suggestion that it is a penalty; the limitation of jurisdiction, which it describes as reservation, does not inflict an incapacity directly on the penitent, which should be the case if there were question of punishment, but the restriction is directly placed on the confessor's power to absolve. The words "nonnullos casus ad suum avocare iudicium" of this canon indicate that the purpose of this limitation of jurisdiction is to bring the penitent before the tribunal of the superior. Just as in civil judgments more serious crimes must be tried before higher courts, in order to safeguard the proper exercise of judicial procedure, so too the safeguarding of ecclesiastical discipline requires that more serious sins should be brought before the tribunals of more learned, prudent and experienced confessors. The fact that a person accused of homicide can not be tried in an ordinary magistrate's court but only in a supreme court may delay the disposal of the case, but this is not to punish the accused, it is merely a means to insure the more expert handling of the case which a crime of such gravity and consequences requires, and as such it is a benefit rather than a punishment for the accused. So in reservation, the fact that an inferior confessor can not absolve, does not prove that the purpose of the delay thus caused is to punish the penitent.

A stronger argument to prove that the primary purpose of reservation is disciplinary and not penal is drawn from the instruction on episcopal reserved cases, issued by the Holy Office on July 13th, 1916, the salient points of which are, with a few significant changes, embodied in the Code.[24] In paragraph 8 of this instruction it is stated: "Above all, Ordinaries should strive to form throughout their dioceses, learned, pious and prudent confessors and to these they should suggest those

[24] S. C. S. Off. inst., 13 Jul. 1916, A. A. S. VIII, 313.

remedies which are adapted to check growing vices and which they themselves would use if the penitents were sent to them. In this way Ordinaries will avoid the hardships inevitable to reservation, which fall on confessor and penitent alike, and, with the help of God, gain the desired effect more gently and more surely."

The last sentence states that if the suggested means are used they will gain the desired effect (i.e., of reservation). Therefore, an examination of the means suggested should disclose the object or purpose of reservation, for from the means one can deduce the end intended. The means suggested are: 1—Ordinaries should strive to form pious, learned and prudent confessors throughout the diocese; 2—They should suggest to these the remedies they themselves would use if the penitents were sent to them.

Surely, these means have not punishment as their object—the penitent will be benefited, rather than punished, by the formation of learned, pious and prudent confessors; nor is the Ordinary to suggest penalties to these but remedies. The entire implication of this paragraph is that if the Ordinary will see to it that specially qualified confessors are formed, he will not have to withdraw certain cases to a higher tribunal since the purpose of reservation, namely the bringing of more serious cases before more qualified judges, is then attained.

This opinion that, per se, the purpose of reservation is disciplinary and not penal did not originate only after the above mentioned instruction of the Holy Office—it may well be termed the traditional opinion and in support of this reference is again made to the words of the Council of Trent: "Magnopere ad Christiani populi disciplinam pertinere sanctissimis Patribus nostris visum est, ut atrociora quaedem et graviora crimina non a quibusvis, sed a summis dumtaxat sacerdotibus absolverentur."[25]

Per se, therefore, the primary purpose of reservation seems

[25] Conc. Trident., Sess. 14, *De Sacr. Poenit.*, C. 7.

to be disciplinary and not penal. We say *per se* because it can not be denied that if a superior expressly wishes to use reservation as a penal measure, he can do so and the primary purpose of his reservation will then be to punish the delinquent. But the contention is that such use of reservation is accidental and secondary and is not verified unless the intention of the superior to so use it is indicated.

5. *The Effect of Ignorance on Reservation*

A question now arises, the solution of which follows from what has been stated concerning the purpose of reservation. Does ignorance of reservation excuse from it? It is important to understand clearly the state of the question. The point at issue is the effect of ignorance *of the reservation,* not the effect of ignorance *of the sinfulness* of the act, nor the effect of *ignorance of the censure*—there is no doubt that ignorance of the sinfulness of the act does away with the reservation, for then no sin has been committed and consequently there is nothing to reserve; likewise ignorance of a censure excuses from it and, therefore, excuses from the reservation of the censure. But the question now under consideration is: granted that a mortal sin, which is reserved, is certainly committed, or that a censure, which is reserved, is certainly incurred, does the fact that the penitent was ignorant *solely of the reservation* excuse him from it?

If the purpose of reservation is disciplinary, ignorance of the reservation does not excuse from it. The person's ignorance that his sin needs the judgment and consideration of an expert confessor does not take away that need, because it is independent of the penitent's ignorance and is created by the serious character of the sin. On the other hand, if the purpose of reservation is penal, ignorance of the reservation would excuse from it because it is unbecoming to punish a delinquent with a penalty which he in no way suspected.

The opinion that, per se, the purpose of reservation is disciplinary and not penal has been already stated and arguments were advanced from the Code, the Instruction of the Holy Office, and the Council of Trent to prove this. It follows, therefore, that ignorance of reservation does not excuse from it, unless the superior has indicated that his object in imposing the reservation is to punish, or unless the superior expressly states that knowledge of the reservation is required in order to be affected by it.

In answer to the question whether or not they who are outside their diocese are affected by the reservations of the place in which they are staying, the Commission for interpreting the Code answered in the affirmative.[26] This confirms the conclusions that ignorance of reservation does not excuse from it, because visitors are, as a general rule, excusably ignorant of the reservations in force in the place they are visiting.

The instruction of the Holy Office, in warning bishops to bring their reservations to the notice of the faithful, added, "for of what avail are they if unknown." This phrase was seized upon as proof that ignorance excuses from reservation, because reservation would serve some purpose if the ignorant were, nevertheless, affected by it. In answer, it is to be noted that the Code omits the phrase and, that paragraph 8 of the very same instruction weakens this argument by its clear indication of the disciplinary character of reservation. The query in the instruction may be justified on the ground that, if knowledge of reservation is not had, it would not have any deterrent force until the sin was confessed.

Before the publication of the Code, the question of the effect of ignorance was greatly disputed by canonists and theologians.[27] In the works that have appeared since the publication of the Code:

[26] Pont. Com. ad CC. auth. interpret., 24 Nov. 1920, A. A. S. XII, 575.

[27] Sanchez, *De Matrimonio,* lib. IX, disp. XXXII,, 15–18; De Lugo, *De Sacr. Poenitentiæ,* disp. XX, sect. II, No. 10; Diana, tract V, resol. XXXVIII, No. 1; Laymann, lib. V, tract VI, Cap. XI, No. 2; Concina, lib. II, cap. VI, 1–10; St. Alphonsus, II, 580; D'Annibile, I, 343; Gury-Ballerini, II, 571.

Genicot-Salsmans[28] hold that ignorance of reservation does not excuse from it unless the reserver explicitly or implicitly excepts those who are ignorant of the reservation. The reason assigned is that, in the Code, reservation has not a penal character.

Vermeersch-Creusen also hold that ignorance of reservation does not excuse from incurring it:[29] "Quaeri consuevit utrum necne ignorantia poenitentem a reservatione excuset. Attenta genuina notione reservationis, quae maturiori iudicio causas graviores subdit, ita ut iurisdictionem inferioris limitet nec inter poenas canonicas numeretur, responsio certo negativa danda videtur. Quod declaratione mox allegata de peregrinis non parum confirmatur. Proprias enim alienae diocesis reservationes hi plerumque ignorant, nec huius ligantur; et tamen simplex confessarius eosdem per se a casibus reservatis absolvere posse, sine ulla distinctione est negatum. Nondum tamen extrinsecam probabilitatem sententiae benigniores reicere audemus."

Ferreres distinguishes—if the sin is reserved without censure he holds ignorance of the reservation does not excuse from it; if it is a case of reserved censure ignorance does excuse from the reservation but he gives as the reason "quia huiusmodi casus papalis reservantur propter censuram, a quo excusat ignorantia"[30] and this indicates that Ferreres here refers to ignorance of censure rather than ignorance of reservation of the censure.

Farrugia[31] summarizes the conflicting opinions and reasons advanced by theologians before the Code and favors the opinion that ignorance of the reservation of a sin reserved *ratione sui* excuses from the reservation.

Prümmer[32] affirms that ignorance of the reservation of a sin

[28] II, 309.
[29] II, 99.
[30] II, 393.
[31] No. 11.
[32] III, 290.

reserved *ratione sui* does not excuse from the reservation but it does excuse in the case of a reserved censure. It is again evident, from the reason given by Prümmer for this latter opinion that he here refers to ignorance of censure rather than ignorance of reservation.

Noldin,[33] Tanquerey,[34] and Sabbetti-Barrett[35] hold practically the same opinion as Prümmer, while Arregui[36] states that it is at least probable that ignorance of reservation which is not crass or supine, excuses from the reservation of a sin, *ratione sui* thereby indicating that this author believes that reservation is always penal.

In conclusion it seems that it is certain that ignorance of *reservation* whether of the reservation of a sin reserved *ratione sui* or of the reservation of a censure does not excuse from the reservation. It appears that the opposite opinion lacks intrinsic probability and it is doubtful whether it is even extrinsically probable.

[33] III, 416.
[34] I, 250.
[35] Page 752.
[36] Page 392.

II. RESERVATION OF SIN "RATIONE SUI"

Before proceeding to examine canons 893 to 900, it may be well to give a general idea of the matter contained in them. Too much stress can not be laid on the fact that this section of the Code, per se, legislates only for reserved sins, and does not legislate, except in a passing way, for reserved censures. In proof of this attention is called to the significant title of this section, "De reservatione *peccatorum,*" and if this is not sufficient to convince, the fact can be conclusively established from canon 893, § 3: "Quod attinet ad reservationem censurarum, servetur praescriptum canon 2246, 2247."

Canon 893 describes a reserved case and determines who possess the power to establish reservations; canon 894 sets forth the only sin reserved *ratione sui* to the Holy See; canon 895 determines the procedure to be observed by Local Ordinaries when establishing reservations, and canon 896 the procedure to be observed by religious superiors; canon 897 determines, in a positive way, what sins may be reserved, while canon 898 does so in a negative way; canon 898 describes what Ordinaries should do after making reservations, and determines to whom faculties to absolve from episcopal reservations should be granted, or are granted *ipso iure;* canon 900 determines when all reservation of sin ceases.[1]

1. *The Power to establish Reservations and the Manner in Which It Is To Be Exercised*

Although the Council of Trent expressly mentioned only the Pope and Bishops in connection with the right to establish reservations, the term "bishop" was interpreted to mean in-

[1] Blat, Lib. III, pars. I, 256.

ferior prelates, who possessed quasi-episcopal jurisdiction.[2] Many canonists also extended the right to establish reservations to pastors as regards simple priests or chaplains, on the ground that pastors possessed ordinary jurisdiction in the internal forum which they could delegate to these chaplains.[3] These authors noted, however, that it was not customary for pastors to use this faculty, and Cardinal de Lugo added that the reservation made by a pastor, would not affect those who heard confessions in virtue of jurisdiction received from the Bishop.[4]

The present law is:

Qui ordinario iure possunt audiendi confessiones potestatem concedere aut ferre censuras, possunt quoque, excepto Vicario Capitulari et Vicario Generali sine mandato speciali, nonnullos casus ad suum avocare iudicium, inferioribus absolvendi potestatem limitantes.[5]

They therefore, who by ordinary power, can grant jurisdiction to hear confessions, with the exception of the Vicar Capitular and the Vicar General, unless the latter has a special mandate, can also summon some cases to their own tribunal by limiting the absolving power of inferiors.

Those who have ordinary power, i.e., power attached by law to an office,[6] to grant jurisdiction to hear confessions, are the Ordinaries of the places in which the confessions are heard, and the superiors of exempt, clerical religious for their defined subjects.[7] Canon 198 sets forth who are Ordinarii Loci, namely the Pope, a residential Bishop, an Abbot or Prelate Nullius and their Vicars General, an Administrator, a Vicar and Prefect Apostolic and, finally those who take the place of these e.g., the Vicar Capitular etc. Since canon 893 expressly

[2] Benedict XIV, *De Synodo Dioecesana,* lib. V, cap. IV, No. II.
[3] Saurez, disput. XXIX, sect. I, No. 7; De Lugo, disput. XX, sect. I, No. 2.
[4] Ibidem.
[5] Canon 893.
[6] Canon 197.
[7] Canons 874, § 1 and 875, § 2.

denies the power to reserve sins to the Vicar Capitular and the Vicar General, unless the latter has a special mandate, and canon 896 restricts the reserving power in exempt clerical orders, to the Superior General, or Abbot of an independent monastery, this leaves the following with the power to reserve: The Pope for the whole Church, the residential Bishop, the Abbot or Prelate Nullius, the Apostolic Administrator, the Vicar and Prefect Apostolic, for their respective territories, and, in exempt clerical orders, the Superior General and Abbot of an independent monastery, for their respective subjects.

National and Provincial councils can reserve sins for the territory they represent. It is now certain that a pastor cannot reserve sins because he cannot, by ordinary power, grant jurisdiction to others to hear confessions.[8]

Before the instruction "Cum Experientia," issued by the Holy Office on July 13th, 1916, there was no positive legislation prescribing the manner in which local Ordinaries should establish reservations.[9] The Council of Trent had cautioned that reservation was to be used very prudently and a letter of the Congregation of Bishops and Regulars had repeated this warning.[10] Canonists advised that reservations should be established in Synod for three principal reasons: First, in order to insure the cautious use of this power, it was expedient that the Ordinary should consult the more experienced priests of the diocese and a synod was the best means of doing this; secondly, in order that the ordinary power of pastors should not be restricted without their knowledge; the third reason they advanced was that a reservation made in synod was a true and proper law, and therefore perpetual, while if established outside of synod, unless the contrary was stated, it was considered only a precept.[11]

---

[8] Pont. Com. ad CC. auth. interpret., 16 Oct. 1919; A. A. S. XI, 477.

[9] Irish Theological Quarterly, XII, 3.

[10] Conc. Trident., Sess. XIV, *De Sacra. Poenit.*, c. 7; S. C. Ep. et Reg., litt. 26 Nov. 1602.

[11] Benedict XIV, *De Synodo Dioecesana,* lib. V, cap. IV, No. III.

To insure the cautious use of the power to reserve, the "Cum Experientia declared: "Meminerint ante omnia Rmi. Ordinarii casuum conscientiae reservationes 'ad destructionem munitionum', iuxta dictum Apostoli, ad removenda scilicet obstacula quae saluti animarum non communi impedimento sunt, esse dirigendas; ideoque, generatim loquendo, extraordinario huic remedio manus ne velint apponere nisi, re in synodo dioecesana discussa, vel, extra synodum, auditis Capitulo Cathedrali et aliquot ex probatioribus ac prudentioribus suae dioecesis animarum curatoribus, de vera reservationis necessitate aut utilate in Domino convincatur."[12]

The wording of this paragraph is practically embodied in canon 895 of The Code:

Locorum Ordinarii peccata ne reservent, nisi, re in Synodo dioecesana discussa, vel extra Synodum auditis Capitulo cathedrali et aliquot ex prudentioribus ac probatioribus suae dioecesis animarum curatoribus, vera reservationis necessitas aut utilitas comprobata fuerit.

According to present law, then, Local Ordinaries should not reserve sins unless they ascertain the true necessity or utility of such reservation, and to do this they should follow one or the other of the two alternatives prescribed in the Code—either discuss the matter in diocesan synod, or consult the Cathedral chapter and some of the more prudent and qualified priests of the diocese. The Ordinary is free to select either of the two methods. In this country diocesan consultors are equivalent to the Cathedral chapter and consequently, they are to be consulted by the Ordinary if he chooses this method.[13]

Are the requirements of this canon necessary for the validity or only for the liceity of the reservation? Whenever the law determines that a superior needs the consent or consultation of some persons to act, the following rules obtain: if consent is required, the superior acts invalidly against the vote

[12] S. C. S. Off., instr. 13 July 1916, par. 1, A. A. S. VIII, 313.
[13] Canon 427.

of these persons; if only consultation is demanded, e.g., by such phrases as "de consilio consultorum" or "audito capitulo, parocho, etc," it is sufficient for the validity of the action that the superior consults these persons; he is not bound to follow their advice.[14] At first sight, it would appear that the consultation required by canon 895 is necessary for validity, especially in view of the fact that the exact phrase "audito capitulo," used as an example in canon 105 is found in canon 895.[15] However, it is by no means conclusive that in canon 895 "ius statuit Superiorem ad agendum indigere. . . .consilio"[16] because in the corresponding section of the Instruction, which is the basis of this canon, there is plainly question only of liceity. In view of this and of the strict interpretation which should be given to a restriction of the power of the Ordinary it seems at least probable that the consultation is necessary only for liceity. It is certain that an Ordinary would act validly if he acted contrary to the advice given him, and even if the discussion of the matter in synod convinces him that the necessity or utility of the reservation is not evident, he would act validly if he establishes the reservation. Ultimate judgment as to the sufficiency of the indications for the utility of some reservation is left to him.

The old legislation governing the establishment of reservations by religious superiors was contained in the Constitution "Sanctissimus" of Clement VIII.[17] This Constitution specified eleven cases, and religious superiors were ordered to confine their reservations to these.[18] The eleven cases were: 1—Apostasia a religione, etiam retento habitu; 2—Nocturna ac furtiva e monasterio egressio; 3—Veneficia, incantationes et sortilegia; 4—Proprietas contra votum paupertatis, quae sit

[14] Canon 105.
[15] Blat., lib. III pars I, 261.
[16] Canon 105.
[17] Clement VIII, decr. *Sanctissimus,* 26 May 1593; Cod. Iur. Can. Fontes, 177.
[18] Blat, lib. III, pars. I, 262.

peccatum mortale; 5—Furtum mortale de rebus monasterii; 6—Lapsus carnis voluntarius opere consummatus; 7—Iuramentum falsum in iudicio legitimo; 8—Procuratio, consilium vel auxilium ad abortum foetus animati, etiam effectu non secuto; 9—Occisio vel vulneratio seu gravis percussio cuiuscunque personae; 10—Falsificatio manus vel sigilli officialium monasterii; 11—Malitiosum impedimentum, retardatio aut aperitio litterarum a Superioribus ad inferiores, vel ab inferioribus ad Superiores.

From among these eleven cases superiors could reserve as many as they judged useful. They could not reserve a sin not contained in this list, unless they discussed the matter with, and received the consent of, the General Chapter, in a case for the whole order, or the Provincial Chapter, in a case for the province.

Canon 896 gives the new law on reservations for exempt clerical religious:

Inter Superiores religionis clericalis exemptae unus Superior generalis, et in monasteriis sui iuris Abbas, cum proprio cuiusque Consilio, peccata, ut supra, subditorum reservare possunt, firmo praescripto canon 518, § 1, 519.

Only the Superior General, and the Abbot of an independent monastery, among the superiors of exempt clerical religious, with their respective Councils, can reserve the sins of their subjects. These subjects include, not only the novices and professed members of the community, but all others who live in the religious house day and night, whether as servants, students, guests or convalescents. [19]

The saving clause referring to canons 518, § 1 and 519, inserted in this canon, practically strips reservation of its force in a religious community. The first of these canons prescribes that in every clerical order or congregation confessors should be appointed for each house, with power, if there is question of exempt religious, to absolve from the cases reserved by the

[19] Canons 875, § 1 and 514.

religious superior. In virtue of the other canon referred to, a religious, for the peace of his conscience, may go to confession to a priest not specifically designated to hear confessions in the religious house, but approved by the Local Ordinary, and this priest can absolve from sins and censures reserved by the religious superior.

The phrase "cum proprio cuisque Consilio" gives rise to some difficulty. Does it mean merely consultation or must the consent of the Council be obtained, and is this consultation or consent necessary for validity or only for liceity? Vermeersch interprets the phrase to mean that the Superior must merely consult the Council and he bases his interpretation on the parallel passage in the preceeding canon, which requires the Ordinary merely to consult the Chapter. [20] Blat holds that the phrase implies either consultation or consent, depending on whether the constitution of the order gives a deliberative or consultive vote in the matter.[21]

2. *The Number and Quality of Reserved Sins*

As in the previous matter the Code incorporates the legislation of the "Cum Experentia" on the number and quality of the sins which may be reserved. [22]

Casus reservandi sint pauci omnino, tres scilicet vel, ad summum, quotuor ex gravioribus tantum et atrocioribus criminibus externis specifice determinatis; ipsa vero reservatio ne ultra in vigore maneat, quam necesse sit ad publicum aliquod inolitum vitium exstirpandum et collapsam forte christianam disciplinam instaurandam.[23]

Reserved cases should be as few as possible, and the law expressly determines that the maximum number should not exceed four. This applies not only to Episcopal reservations

[20] Vermeersch-Creusen, II, 177.
[21] Blat, Lib. III, pars. I, 263.
[22] Paragraphs 2, 3 and 4.
[23] Canon 897.

as did the "Cum Experientia"; the canon is general and therefore includes the reservations of religious superiors.

Suppose a Local Ordinary or Religious Superior reserves more than four sins, would the added reservations be valid? This canon does not contain an express or equivalent invalidating clause and consequently, if Superiors reserved more than four sins, they would act unlawfully but validly. [24]

The generic term "casus" is used in this canon. Does this mean that both reserved sins and reserved censures are included and that Superiors are limited to three or four cases including both sins and censures? The term "casus" here refers only to reserved sins for the following reasons: 1—This section of the Code is dealing only with reserved sins as its title and canon 893, § 3 clearly indicate; 2—The same matter dealt with in this canon in connection with reserved sins, is dealt with again in canon 2246 in connection with reserved censures; 3—In the very next canon, (can. 898), the Code wishes to include reserved censures and therefore expressly states so, ("etiam ratione censurae reservata) thus indicating that this section of the Code, per se, refers only to reserved sins.

After determining how many sins may be reserved, the canon describes what kind of sins these should be, namely from the more grave and atrocious crimes, specifically determined. Reservation is a "res odiosa" and consequently these various qualifications are to be taken strictly. The sin must be mortal both by reason of its matter and malice (i. e., subjectively and objectively), but over and above this, it should be grave and atrocious.[25] Since venial sins are not necessary matter for confession they cannot be reserved in the strict sense of the term because the penitent cannot be forced to seek sacramental absolution from them. But, absolutely speaking, they could be reserved in a relative way, that is the Superior could restrict jurisdiction to absolve from venial sins so that if they were submitted by the penitent, the confessor could not absolve them

[24] Canon 11.

[25] Noldin, III, 361.

directly. But the policy of the Church has always been against reserving not only venial sins but even mortal sins of ordinary malice.[26] In determining when a mortal sin is more grave and atrocious, much will depend on circumstances and the prudent judgment of the Superior and his advisers. Evidently if a person is excused from mortal sin for any reason, there is no reservation.

The sin reserved should be external. Again this is not necessary *ex natura rei*, because, absolutely speaking, a Superior could withhold jurisdiction to absolve from an internal sin, and, if he expressly did so, the reservation would be unlawful but valid. The policy of the Church has always been against the reservation of internal sins because it is not expedient and would prove more of a danger than an aid to the eternal salvation of souls.[27] It is the teaching of moral theologians that in order to be affected by reservation, the sin must be grave as an external sin, so that if the external act is only objectively a venial sin, the reservation would not be incurred, no matter how great the internal malice or guilt might be.[28] Thus, for example, if murder of a cleric is a reserved sin, a person who only succeeded in striking him lightly would not be affected by the reservation. Moreover, the external sin should be consummated—a merely attempted external sin will not incur the reservation unless the express statement of the Superior indicates that he reserved the attempted action.

The sin reserved should be "specifice determinatis." By this phrase the canon safeguards its initial legislation that only three or four sins are to be reserved for, if the superiors did not have to specifically determine these, they could include any number of sins under three or four undetermined species.[29]

The last part of canon 897 sets forth a rather general principle to determine how long a reservation of sin should remain

[26] Lehmkuhl, II, 523.

[27] De Lugo, disput. XX, sect. II, No. 13; Suarez, disput. XXIX, sect. III, No. 3; Benedict XIV, *De Synodo Dioecesana,* lib. V, cap. V. No. V.

[28] Lehmkuhl, II, 524.

[29] Vermeersch-Creusen, II, 178.

in force. Reservation should not remain in force any longer than is necessary for the extirpation of some grave public crime and the restoration of Christian discipline. An evident deduction from the subjunctive "maneat" is that a reservation does not cease *ipso iure* when its end has been attained, but its removal requires action on the part of the Superior, so that it remains in force until he supplies the restricted jurisdiction.

The Code not only determines in a positive way but also in a negative way what sins may be reserved:

Prorsus ab iis peccatis sibi reservandis omnes abstineant quae iam sint Sedi Apostolicae etiam ratione censurae reservata, et regulariter ab iis quoque quibus censura, etsi nemini reservata, a iure imposita sit. [30]

Ordinaries should refrain entirely from reserving to themselves sins which have already been reserved by the Holy See, even though reserved *ratione censurae.* [31] Suppose an Ordinary did reserve to himself a sin already reserved by the Holy See, would his action be valid? Some authors hold his action would be unlawful but valid; others hold it would be both unlawful and invalid. [32] In answering the question it seems a distinction should be made between a sin which is reserved by the Holy See to itself, and a sin which is reserved by the Holy See, to an inferior Ordinary. In the first case it seems that a bishop would act both unlawfully and invalidly in reserving the same sin to himself because reservation to the Holy See involves the withdrawal of jurisdiction from all inferior tribunals. The practical result would be that if a bishop so acted a confessor who had power to absolve from the Papal case, could use it, despite the bishop's attempt to reserve the case. But if the sin is reserved by the Holy See to an inferior Ordinary, this does not involve the withdrawal of jurisdiction from the inferior tribunal (i. e. to whom the sin is reserved),

[30] Canon 898.

[31] Canon 2247, § 1; S. C. S. Off. instr. 13 Jul. 1916, par. 4.

[32] Suarez, disput. XXXI, Sect. IV, Nos. 25–26; De Lugo, disput. XX, Sect. VIII, No. 151; Ballerini-Palmeri, V, 514.

and consequently it seems probable that these Ordinaries would act validly, though unlawfully if they reserved the same sin to themselves, because canon 898 does not contain an express or equivalent invalidating clause.

As a rule, Ordinaries should also refrain from reserving sins to which a censure has already been attached by the Holy See, even though the censure is not reserved. The word "regulariter" indicates that this class of cases is not completely withdrawn from the reserving power of Ordinaries, and consequently the latter would always act validly and sometimes even lawfully, if they did reserve these to themselves. However, the very fact that the general Legislator has considered these cases, and has imposed a penalty, without reserving it, indicates that as a general rule, reservation of these cases is not necessary.

The only sin which has been reserved *ratione sui* to the Holy See is the false accusation of an innocent priest, of the crime of solicitation:

Unicum peccatum ratione sui reservatum Sanctae Sedi est falsa delatio, qua sacerdos innocens accusatur de crimine sollicitationis apud iudices ecclesiasticos.[33]

The term *ratione sui* in this canon indicates that it is the sin which is here directly and immediately reserved. The sin reserved is "falsa delatio," and consequently to incur the reservation the accusation must be false according to the conscience of the delinquent and truly calumnious. This false accusation must be made against a "Sacerdos innocens" and hence, since the word "Sacerdos" is unqualified, it does not matter whether or not the priest is a confessor. The false accusation must be "de crimine sollicitationis" which is defined in the following words of the Constitution "Sacramentum Poenitentiae" of Benedict XIV,[34] "Mandamus—ut—praecedent—contra omnes,

[33] Canon 894.

[34] Benedict XIV, const. *Sacramentum Poenitentiæ,* 1 June 1741, par. I, doc. V in Code.

et singulos sacerdotes—, qui aliquem poenitentem, quaecumque illa persona sit, vel in actu sacramentalis confessionis vel ante, vel immediate post confessionem, vel occasione, aut praetextu confessionis, vel etiam extra occasionem confessionis in confessionali sive in alio loco ad confessiones audiendas destinato, aut electo, cum simulatione audiendi ibidem confessionem, ad inhonesta, et turpia sollicitare, vel provocare, sive verbis, sive signis, sive nutibus, sive tactu, sive per scripturam aut tunc aut post legendam, tentaverint, aut cum eis illicitos, et inhonestos sermones, vel tractatus temerario ausu habuerint."

The final condition necessary to incur this reserved sin is that the false accusation should be made "apud Iudices ecclesiasticos." Because of the principle "odiosa sunt restringenda," this phrase is to be interpreted strictly and will only be verified when a canonical accusation is made; if the denunciation is made anonymously, or if the name of the accuser is not given in full, a document would not have juridical force and the person would not fall under the present law.

It is to be noted that canon 2363 attaches to this crime an excommunication, reserved *speciali modo* to the Holy See. While the terminology of these two canons is not exactly the same, they fundamentally legislate on one and the same sin. In some respects, the terms used in canon 894 are wider than those used in canon 2363, in others they are narrower. For example, canon 894 uses the wider term "sacerdos innocens" as compared with "confessarius" in canon 2363; yet canon 894 uses the restricted "apud iudices ecclesiasticos" as compared with the wider term "apud superiores" in canon 2363. Despite these differences it is possible for a delinquent to violate both canons by one and the same act. The accidental differences in the terminology are to be accounted for in the manner in which the Code was compiled rather than the deliberate intention of the legislator to constitute different objective acts by changing the wording of both canons. The saving clause "firmo praescripto canon 894," inserted in canon 2363, makes it certain that both canons refer to one and the same sin and crime. It is difficult to see what other meaning this phrase can have than that the sin of false denunciation remains reserved *ratione sui* even after the reserved censure has been absolved.

This sin reserved *ratione sui* and all the censures both reserved and unreserved, established by the Holy See, and found in the fifth book of The Code, should be kept in mind by inferior Ordinaries, when establishing reservations.

Once they have made reservations, Local Ordinaries should see to it that knowledge of these is brought to the attention of their subjects, by means best suited to accomplish this.[85] The utility of reservations would be diminished, if the people did not know of them. This does not mean that reservations intended only for a special class or group, e.g., priests, must be brought to the attention of the general public. It is left to the judgment of the Ordinary to select the means best suited to bring notice of his reservations to his subjects. After making reservations, Ordinaries should uphold them and not render them merely nominal by granting faculties freely and indiscriminately to absolve from them.

[85] Canon 899, § 1.

3. *Absolution From Sins Reserved "Ratione Sui"*

In the instruction "Cum Experientia" it was stated: "Mens tamen est S. Congregationis ut huiusmodi absolvendi facultas habitualiter impertiatur saltem Canonico Poenitentiario, etiam Ecclesiae Collegiatae et Vicariis foraneis eorumve vices gerentibus, addita his ultimis, praesertim in locis dioecesis a sede episcopali remotioribus, etiam facultate subdelegandi toties quoties confessarios sui districtus, si et quando pro urgentiori aliquo determinato casu ad eos recurrant."

The Code extends this in connection with the power of the Canon Penitentiary:

At huismodi absolvendi facultas ipso iure competit canonico poenitentiario ad norman can. 301, § 1, et habitualiter impertiatur saltem vicariis foraneis, addita, praesertim in locis dioecesis a sede episcopali remotioribus, facultate subdelegandi toties quoties confessarios sui districtus, si et quando pro urgentiore aliquo determinato casu ad eos recurrant.[1]

Before the Code then, the Canon Penitentiary did not possess, *ipso iure,* faculties to absolve from episcopal cases but he was to be habitually delegated these faculties. The Code extends this and declares that the Canon Penitentiary, whether of a Cathedral or a Collegiate Church, possesses, *ipso iure,* the power to absolve from cases reserved to the Bishop. Moreover the word "Episcopo," in canon 401, may be taken to mean cases reserved to the bishop or by the bishop. The Canon Penitentiary may exercise this power on externs in his territory and on diocesans outside of the limits of the diocese,[2] but cannot delegate this power. While the Code grants an

[1] Canon 899, § 1.
[2] Canon 401, § 1.

extension of power to the Canon Penitentiary it makes no such extension in the power of deans. They now, as before, do not possess the power *ipso iure,* to absolve from episcopal reservations, but habitual faculties should be granted to them by the Ordinary, and if they are far removed from the episcopal see they should be given the added faculty of subdelegating when confessors of their districts seek jurisdiction for some determined, urgent case.

Part 3 of canon 899 states that pastors, and those who are equivalent to them in law, possess, *ipso iure,* the power to absolve from episcopal cases during the time in which the Easter duty urges. Those who are equivalent to Parochi are quasi-parochi, that is those in charge of a division of a Vicariate or Prefecture Apostolic, and those who take the place of Parochi with full parochial power;[3] all of these are included in this canon but the power extends only to the cases which a bishop has reserved to himself and during the time for fulfilling the Easter precept. By common law, the time for fulfilling the Easter precept extends from Palm Sunday to Low Sunday, but Local Ordinaries, if circumstances require, may anticipate this time and have it begin earlier, though not earlier than the fourth Sunday of Lent; they may also extend it but not beyond Trinity Sunday.[4] If the Local Ordinary should lengthen the regular time, the faculty would also extend to the time determined by him. It is not necessary that the confession be made for the purpose of fulfilling the Easter duty; this entire time is privileged so that even if one who has already made his Easter duty commits a sin reserved by the Bishop, and goes to confession again during this time, he could be absolved by those mentioned above.[5]

Canon 899 also grants to Missioners the power to absolve from episcopal cases during the time they are engaged in giv-

[3] Canon 451, § 2.
[4] Canon 859, § 2.
[5] Vermeersch-Creusen, II, 180, 3.

ing missions. Since this is a favorable law, retreat masters may also be included because missions and retreats are practically identical.

4. *The Cessation of Reservation of Sins Ipso Iure*

In the "Cum Experientia,"[6] five cases were grouped together in which, either reservation of sin ceased *ipso iure*, or faculties were granted *ipso iure* to absolve. The Code has retained these five cases but a comparison of its statement and that of the Instruction forces one to conclude that the Code introduces some changes of importance. The Instruction grouped all five cases together, but the Code has separated them in a significant manner. It places two of them, namely absolution by pastors, and their equivalents, during Easter time, and of missioners, under canon 899, which canon, like the Instruction, refers only to cases which the Bishop has reserved to himself. The Code separates the other three cases from the two just mentioned and holds them over in order to devote a special canon to them. In this separate canon it omits the qualifying phrase "Locorum Ordinarii" found in Canon 899, and substitutes the absolutely general heading, "Quaevis reservatio omni vi caret." One is, therefore, forced to conclude that canon 900 refers to all reservations of sin, whether episcopal, religious or papal. Some authors do not admit this and restrict it to episcopal reservations,[7] and their principal reason is that the "Cum Experientia," on which this canon is based, referred only to episcopal cases. But it should be remembered that the Instruction constitutes the old legislation on this matter; where its statement agrees with that of the Code, all well and good in using it to interpret the Code, but when they differ, it is the Code which constitutes existing law.[8] And on this point the Code and the Instruction do differ—the Instruc-

[6] Paragraph 7.
[7] Blat. Lib. III, pars. I, 268.
[8] Canon 6, Nos. 2 and 3.

tion reads "quaevis Ordinariorum reservatio," while the Code makes the absolutely general statement "Quaevis reservatio."

While canon 900 is general and refers to papal as well as episcopal reservation, by this is meant all reservation of sin—it does not refer to reservation of censure. In proof of this, it is necessary to repeat the arguments cited so often showing that this section of the Code deals, per se, with reserved sins and not with reserved censures, namely the title of this section "De reservatione peccatorum," the statement of § 3 of canon 893, and the fact that the matter treated in canon 900 in reference to reserved sins can be found in canon 2247, § 2, and § 2254, in reference to reserved censures.

With these distinctions in mind let us examine the canon. It states that all reservations ceases in the following cases:

1. When they, who are unable to leave their home because of sickness, make their confession, and also when betrothed confess in preparation for marriage. "Aegroti" includes not only those who are suffering from some internal disease but all who are physically incapacitated e.g., by old age, an injured foot, etc. Grave illness is not required, but merely that illness which is sufficient to necessitate confinement to the house. This canon can be applied in the case of sick religious, even when confessors live in the same house.[9]

"Sponsi" includes all who go to confession in proximate preparation for marriage, whether they are formally engaged by canonical sponsalia or not.

2. Reservation of sin ceases also when, in a particular case, faculties to absolve are sought from, and refused by, a competent superior; it likewise ceases as often as, in the prudent judgment of the confessor, faculties for some particular case cannot be sought from a competent superior without grave inconvenience to the penitent, or without danger of violating the seal.

If therefore, a confessor applies to a competent superior for

[9] Vermeersch-Creusen, II, 179, 3.

faculties to absolve from a reserved sin, and the superior refuses to grant these, the reservation ceases *ipso iure,* regardless of the motive of the superior in refusing to grant the faculty. After such denial the sin is no longer reserved and the confessor can go ahead and absolve from it. In keeping with the wide interpretation to be given a favorable law, "legitimus superior" includes country deans when they have habitual faculties over episcopal cases with the added faculty of delegating others in particular cases so that if a country dean possessing this power refused the application of a confessor for faculties to absolve from episcopal reservation the reservation would cease *ipso iure.*

Reservation also ceases as often as the confessor prudently judges that he cannot ask for faculties without grave inconvenience to the penitent; examples of such grave inconvenience would be, if the penitent would suffer loss of reputation, if it would be very difficult for the penitent to return to confession, if he could not omit celebrating Mass or receiving Communion without causing scandal, if the penitent would feel it a grave hardship to remain in the state of mortal sin during the time necessary to obtain the faculty to absolve. While confessors should not be too easily led into believing that reservation has ceased, yet when it is clear that the circumstances that do away with reservation are verified they should not hesitate to absolve.

3. All reservation ceases outside of the territory of the reserver, even though the penitent purposely left to obtain absolution. In the case of a reservation established by common law and in force everywhere, evidently no matter where the penitent goes he is in the territory of the reserver and hence such reservation binds everywhere. But this is not true of particular reservations. If a sin is reserved in a certain diocese and is not reserved in the adjoining diocese, a penitent may go from the former to the latter and be absolved by any confessor. Suppose a penitent goes from one diocese where the

sin is reserved to another diocese where it is also reserved, is he affected by the reservation in this second diocese or has the reservation ceased because he left the territory of the first diocese? Two principles are to be kept in mind in dealing with the question of the relation of peregrini to episcopal reservations. The first is that peregrini are absolved by virtue of jurisdiction derived from the Ordinary of the place in which the confessions are heard. [10] The second principle to be kept in mind is that reservation directly affects the confessor. Combining these two principles it logically follows that peregrini are affected by the reservation in force in the place in which they make their confession. Since they are absolved by virtue of jurisdiction derived from or through the Local Ordinary of the place where the confession is heard, and since he has directly limited the power of the confessor whom the peregrinus approaches, it follows that this confessor cannot absolve a peregrinus from a sin reserved in the diocese any more than he could absolve one of his own diocesans from that sin, so that, in practice, peregrini are in exactly the same position as diocesans in reference to reservation of sin. The Commission for Interpreting the Code was asked whether or not *peregrini* are affected by the reservation in force in the diocese in which they are staying, and answered in the affirmative. [11]

If, then, a person commits a sin in his own diocese, and thereafter leaves his own diocese and goes to confession in another diocese, where the sin is not reserved, he can be absolved by any confessor because "extra territorium reservantis, etiamsi dumtaxat ad absolutionem obtinendam penitens ex eo discesserit, quaevis reservatio omni vi caret." [12] But if the sin is also reserved in the diocese to which he goes, he is affected by the reservation and cannot be absolved by a simple confessor in this second diocese because the latter's jurisdiction has been limited, thus depriving him of power to absolve from

[10] Canons 874, § 1 and 881.
[11] Pont. Com. ad CC. auth. interpret., 24 Nov. 1920, A. A. S. XII, 575.
[12] Canon 900, § 3.

the reserved sin regardless of whether the penitent is a peregrinus or a diocesan. One may say: "but canon 900 expressly states that all reservation ceases outside the territory of the reserver." This is true but in the case we are considering, the peregrinus is not really "extra territorium reservantis"—he has left the territory of one reserver and has entered the territory of another to whom he is subject in the Sacrament of Penance so that he is really "intra territorium reservantis." If, for example, a subject of the Diocese of Baltimore commits a sin reserved in that diocese, and then travels to the Diocese of New York to go to confession, he can be absolved by any confessor in New York, provided the sin is not also reserved there. If the sin is also reserved in New York, he cannot be absolved there by a simple confessor, not by reason of the reservation in Baltimore, but by reason of the reservation in New York. In all cases of reservation of sin, the thing to be considered is the place where the penitent goes to confession; the place where the sin was committed does not affect the case.

In danger of death, any priest, even though not approved to hear confessions, can validly and lawfully absolve any penitent from any sin or censure, whether reserved or not.[13] The only exception, in danger of death, is that a priest cannot licitly absolve his accomplice if another priest can be had. Absolution in danger of death will be discussed in greater detail in the section on reserved censures.

Reservation also ceases after a valid absolution given by one who has ordinary or delegated power to absolve from the reserved sin. Therefore a simple confessor can absolve from reserved sins, if they are again submitted to the keys after the penitent has already received direct absolution from them.[14]

It is probable reservation ceases, if, in an invalid or sacrilegious confession, the reserved sin is submitted to a confessor who has power to absolve from it, because a competent superior has then passed judgment on it and has given a penance and an

---

[13] Canon 882.

[14] Noldin, III, 364.

instruction for it; in this case the penitent is bound to fulfill this penance even though the confession is invalid.[15] It is also probable that reservation ceases after a valid confession made to a confessor who has power over the reserved sin, if the penitent through inculpable forgetfulness fails to confess the reserved sin. Theologians who hold this opinion appeal to the words of absolution "in quantum possum et tu indiges," and argue that the presumption is that the confessor wishes to do everything he can for the penitent, and it is probable that a reserved sin can be indirectly absolved if the confessor, who possesses the necessary faculties wishes to do so when the penitent inculpably omits it in confession.[16]

When a simple confessor absolves from a sin which is doubtfully reserved, it is certain that the absolution is valid, even though, later on, it becomes certain that the sin was reserved; in positive and probable doubt, whether of law or of fact, the Church supplies jurisdiction.[17]

[15] Lehmkuhl, II, 528.
[16] St. Alphonsus, VI, 597.
[17] Canon 209.

III. RESERVED CENSURES AND SINS RESERVED *RATIONE CENSURAE*

It has been pointed out that reserved cases are divided into two classes, namely reserved sins and reserved censures and that as a result of this distinction, the Code logically treats each of these kinds of reservation in a separate and distinct place. Thus far, this dissertation has been devoted to an explanation of the legislation governing the reservation of sin *ratione sui*. We now come to a second class of reserved cases, that is reserved censures and the consequent reservation of sin *ratione censurae*. Legislation governing this class of reserved cases is contained under section II of the fifth book of the Code, and more particularly in canons 2245–2254.

Since reservation of censure is not verified unless the censure is incurred and since the incurring of censure is governed by the laws regulating ecclesiastical punishments, it will be necessary, in order to adequately present the doctrine on reserved censures, to explain the notion of ecclesiastical punishment, and more specifically that of censure, and to indicate the conditions for inflicting censure and the causes or circumstances that excuse from incurring it.

1. *Ecclesiastical Punishment in General*

At the very beginning of the section "De Poenis in genere," the Code sets forth a general principle of public law determining the right of the Church to punish its delinquent subjects.

It is a native and proper right of the Church, independent of any human authority, to punish her delinquent subjects with penalties both spiritual and temporal.[1] This native and proper right of the Church arises from her very nature and end.

[1] Canon 2214.

The Church is a properly so called and truly juridical society; her end is the sanctification of her subjects in order to lead them to eternal salvation. As such a society, she has the right to command her subjects to obey the laws which she establishes for the attainment of this end, and, conversely, her subjects are bound by a strict obligation to render this obedience. If they fail to do so, if they refuse to make use of the means established by the Church for their sanctification, if they refuse to submit to, or execute her decisions, the Church must possess the power to punish them, else she is deprived of a means most necessary to attain the end for which she was instituted and the scandalous influence of those, who could with impunity contumaciously refuse to obey her laws, decisions and enactments, would react on all Christians and ultimately result in the entire overthrow of ecclesiastical, social order. A perfect society has the right, not only to some means necessary to attain its end, but to all means which are useful or necessary and, at the same time, proportionate to this end.

This right of the Church to punish, arising as it does from the nature and end of the Church, is confirmed by Holy Scripture,[2] and has always been asserted by the Church. Pope John XXII, in the Bull "Licet"[3] against the error of Marsilius Patavius, after quoting the words of St. Matthew, XVIII, 17, continues: "Adhuc constat, sicut ibi legitur in Matthaeo, quod si aliquis damnum alicui indebite dederit, illudque per mandatum Ecclesiae emendare, quod Ecclesiae per potestatem a Christo sibi concessam, ipsum ad hoc per excommunicationis sententiam compellere potest, quae quidem est utique coactiva."

In the same Bull, the following proposition of Marsilius is condemned: "Tota Ecclesiae simul iuncta nullum hominem punire potest punitione coactiva nisi concedat hoc imperator." Hence the right of the Church to punish is not the result of

[2] St. Matth., XVI, XVIII, 18; I Corinth., IV, 21; II Corinth., X, 6.

[3] John XXII, const. *Licet,* 23 Oct. 1327, Art. 5; Code Iur. Con. Fontes, I, 38.

concession on the part of civil authority, but is native and proper—"independens a qualibet humana auctoritate."

An ecclesiastical punishment is the privation of some good, inflicted by legitimate authority, to correct the delinquent and to punish the crime.[4] The goods, which the Church may take from her delinquent subjects, are those whose possession and use depend upon her, including temporal as well as spiritual. They consist either of rights instituted by Christ and committed by Him to the care of the Church, as, for example, the Sacraments, or goods which the Church herself procures or grants, such as benefices or patronage, or goods which the Church guards by her laws, such as reputation, liberty, and temporal goods. Since grace, or merit or the sacramental character do not directly depend upon the disposal of the Church, she can not take them away by her punishments.

The ultimate and intrinsic end of ecclesiastical punishment is the conservation and protection of social order in the Church. This end is intrinsic to the very nature of punishment and can not be excluded.[5] The Church may intend many other ends, and, in keeping with her supreme end of providing for the salvation of souls, it is true she especially aims to correct the delinquent and often prefers to consider the criminal rather than the crime. But because of the importance she gives to this end, one should not lose sight of the above mentioned necessary intrinsic end and conclude that it is not present in those punishments which principally tend to correct the delinquent. There is, therefore, a necessary, intrinsic end common to all ecclesiastical punishments, namely, the conservation and protection of social order in the Church. Besides this, the Legislator may propose as a more primary end, in approximate sense, either the correction of the delinquent or the punishment of the crime and the reparation of the injury and the scandal caused by the crime.[6] The principal, proximate end

[4] Canon 2215.
[5] Chelodi, No. 18.
[6] Cerato, cap. I, No. 5, note a; Lega, III, 8.

intended by the Legislator constitutes the basis of one of the most important divisions of ecclesiastical punishments.

By reason of the principal, proximate end intended, the punitive measures used by the Church are divided into: a—Medicinal Punishments or Censures; b—Vindictive Punishments; c—Penal remedies and Penances.[7] Medicinal punishments, or censures, are those which have as their primary, proximate purpose the correction of the delinquent. They are divided into excommunications, suspensions and interdicts.[8] Vindictive punishments are those whose primary, proximate purpose is the public vindication and punishment of the crime, though, secondarily, they also intend the correction of the wrongdoer.[9] Canon 2291 enumerates twelve vindictive punishments, but these do not exhaust the list because the word "praesertim" indicates that the list is not set forth in a taxative way. Penal remedies are measures used to prevent some crime, or to remove some scandal or voluntary occasion of sin. The Code enumerates four penal remedies, monitio, correptio, praeceptum and vigilantia.[10] Penances are imposed in order that the delinquent may escape strict punishment or, having contracted punishment, that he may be absolved or dispensed from it.[11] A list of the principal penances is given in canon 2313. Since only certain kinds of reserved censures give rise to reservation of the connected sin, it will not be necessary to give a more detailed notion of vindictive punishments and penal remedies or penances.

By reason of the manner in which they are inflicted, ecclesiastical punishments are divided into: a—*Latae Sententiae* and b—*Ferendae Sententiae*.[12] A punishment is *latae sententiae* if it is added to a law or precept in such a way that it is incurred by the very fact of the commission of the crime, without any

[7] Canon 2216.
[8] Canon 2255.
[9] Canon 2286.
[10] Canon 2306.
[11] Canon 2312.
[12] Canon 2217, § 1, No. 2; Lega, III, 96.

further action on the part of the superior. A punishment is *ferendae sententiae* if it is inflicted, after the commission of the crime by a judge or superior, that is the commission of the crime does not, ipso facto, inflict a punishment *ferendae sententiae* but action of a superior is required after the commission of the crime.

A declaratory sentence of a punishment *latae sententiae* may be given by a Superior, but this does not inflict the penalty, because the latter was *latae sententiae* and therefore inflicted at the very moment of the commission of the crime—all the declaratory sentence does is to make the crime committed and the penalty, already incurred, judicially manifest, a process which carries with it certain canonical effects. A condemnatory sentence, on the other hand, actually inflicts a punishment *ferendae sententiae.* A delinquent is bound by a punishment *latae sententiae* in each forum, as soon as the crime is committed, yet, before a declaratory sentence, he is excused from observing the punishment in the external forum, if he can not do so without infamy, and, until a declaratory sentence is given, no one can demand the observance of the penalty in the external forum unless the crime is notorious.[13] It is generally left to the prudent judgment of the Superior whether or not to issue a declaratory sentence, although he is obliged to do so upon the request of an interested party, or when the common good demands it,[14] and when such sentence is given it is retroactive, as regards its canonical effects, to the moment the crime was committed.[15] It is now authentically stated that a penalty is always *ferendae sententiae,* unless it is expressly indicated that it is *latae sententiae.*[16]

Another division of penalties, which plays a very important part in the legislation on reserved censures, is that of: a—Punishments *a iure* and b—Punishments *ab homine.* If

[13] Canon 2232, § 1.
[14] Canon 2223, § 4.
[15] Canon 2232, § 2.
[16] Canon 2217, § 2.

a determinate penalty, whether *latae* or *ferendae sententiae*, is established in the law itself it is *a iure;* but if the punishment is imposed by a particular precept or by a condemnatory sentence it is *ab homine.* It is immediately evident that a punishment *ferendae sententiae* may be both *a iure* and *ab homine,* because it may be established in the law itself and inflicted by a condemnatory sentence. In this case, the punishment *ferendae sententiae,* added to the law, is only *a iure* before sentence but after sentence it is both *a iure* and *ab homine,* though it is considered as *ab homine.*[17] A punishment *a iure* is inflicted after the manner of a true law, whether universal or particular, or through a general precept; a punishment *ab homine,* on the other hand, is inflicted through a particular precept or a judicial sentence.[18]

2. *Censures in General*

The name "censura" passed into canon law from Roman Law. "Censores" were appointed in the Roman Republic about the year 311 B. C. It was their duty to watch over the conduct and morals of the various ranks of citizens and reduce nobles, knights and senators from their grades if they committed some grave wrong.[19] The early Church took over this notion of censure in a modified form; solicitously watchful over the conduct of her subjects, she excluded from the enjoyment of the rights of Christians those subjects who disregarded her laws. In the early Church the names of the faithful, who were in communion, were entered on a register (censum), and read at public gatherings and those who were excluded from communion with the faithful were stricken off this list. At this early date, however, no distinction was made between medicinal or vindictive punishments or between the various kinds of censures. The general name "excommunicati" was applied to all who were excluded from participation in the

[17] Canon 2217, § 1, No. 3.
[18] Wernz, VI, 146.
[19] Lega, III, 124.

rights of Christians, whether this exclusion was complete or only partial. It was not until the period of the Decretals that clear distinctions were gradually established between the various kinds of ecclesiastical punishments.[20] In this period a great advance was made in legal science, and, through the distinctions established by commentators and the Scholastics, the term "censure" gradually acquired the definite meaning of excommunication, suspension and interdict. Innocent III, although he used the term to signify punishment in general in the year 1200,[21] when asked, at a later date, what the term meant, answered: "Quaerenti quid per censuram Ecclesiasticam debeat intelligi cum huiusmodi clausulam in nostris litteris apponimus, respondemus quod per eam non solum interdicti, sed suspensionis et excommunicationis sententia valet intelligi ut iudex discretus rerum et personarum circumstantiis indigatis, ferat quam magis viderit expedire."[22] While the term censure thus gradually came to mean excommunication, suspension and interdict, terminology was not yet so exactly defined as to limit its use to medicinal punishments. It was not until the fifteenth century that the distinction of medicinal and vindictive punishments was clearly established.[23]

The first general censure for the universal Church was established in the Second Lateran Council.[24] Many others were gradually established after this and by the XIV century there was a list of some twenty general excommunications, reserved to the Pope and solemnly published at Rome on Holy Thursday of every year, through the Bull "In Coena Domini."[25] An important element influencing the development of the legislation on censures was the Constitution "Ad Vitanda" of Martin V.[26] Prior to this all persons publicly known to be under

[20] Chelodi, No. 31.
[21] C. 13, X, *De Iudiciis,* II, 1.
[22] C. 20, X, *De verborum significatione,* V, 40.
[23] Chelodi, No. 31.
[24] II Lateran Council, (1139), can. 15.
[25] Catholic Encyclopedia, VII, 717.
[26] Martin V, Const. *Ad evitanda,* a 1418; Cod. Iur. Can. Fontes, I, 45.

censure, were to be avoided in religious and civil intercourse. The Constitution of Martin V decreed that only those censured persons were *vitandi* who were expressly declared such. In the course of years the list of censures became so complicated that it was difficult to know what censures were actually in force. To clarify this, Pius IX issued the Constitution "Apostolicae Sedis,"[27] which abrogated many censures *latae sententiae,* modified others, and established a new list of common law censures *latae sententiae* which constituted existing law down to the promulgation of the Code.

In the Code a censure is defined as: "Poena qua homo baptizatus, delinquens et contumax, quibusdam bonis spiritualibus vel spiritualibus adnexas privatur, donec, a contumacia recedens, absolvatur."[28] A censure, therefore, is a species or class of ecclesiastical punishment, distinguished from others by reason of its primary, proximate end—it is inflicted on one who is "delinquens et contumax . . . donec, a contumacia recedens, absolvatur." It is a medicinal punishment; just as medicine is prescribed to break down and cure some serious ailment, so censures are inflicted, primarily, to break down the contumacy of a delinquent, and just as medicine is not prescribed for life or perpetually but only for the period of the disease, so censures are not inflicted perpetually or for a determined time but "donec, a contumacia recedens." Once the delinquent has receded from his contumacy, he has a right to be absolved.[29] Excommunication is always a censure: suspension and interdict may be either censures or vindictive punishments; when they are inflicted for a determined period of time they are vindictive punishments but when they are inflicted for an indetermined period they are censures, and in case of doubt as to whether they are censures or vindictive punishments, they are presumed to be censures.[30]

---

[27] Pius IX, Const. *Apostolicae Sedis,* 12 Oct. 1869; Collectanea, II, 1348.
[28] Canon 2241.
[29] Canon 2248, § 2.
[30] Canon 2255, § 2.

In defining a censure, canon 2241 indicates that it is a punishment inflicted only upon those who are delinquent and contumacious. Canon 2242 declares further the manner in which the person is to be delinquent and contumacious. In order that a crime be punished by censure it should be: a—external; b—grave; c—consummated; d—joined with contumacy. Inasmuch as these are four elements which will determine whether or not a censure is incurred, and consequently whether or not the reservation is incurred, it will be well to examine them in some detail.

In the first place, there must be a crime in the strict sense of the term. A crime, in ecclesiastical law, is an external and morally imputable violation of a law, to which is connected, at least indeterminately, a canonical sanction.[31] The end of the Church is the sanctification of her individual members. These members can be considered under a twofold aspect, namely as so many individuals concerning whose acts and omissions account is to be rendered to God, or, secondly, as banded together to constitute one external society. Viewed under the first aspect, the Church cares for the faithful primarily in the internal forum, where sins are absolved, reserved and punished with congruous penances. Viewed under the second aspect, the Church governs and rules the faithful primarily in the external forum, and in this forum she punishes crimes and guards social order. Sins, then, fall under the jurisdiction of the Church in the internal forum; crimes fall under the jurisdiction of the Church in the external forum. Any evil action or omission is a sin; it becomes a crime only if it violates some penal law of the Church. Hence, every crime is a sin but not every sin is a crime. A crime is something external, and consequently a violation of a penal law, committed only internally, is a sin but it is not a crime. An external violation, however, may be absolutely occult or unknown, yet it is a crime in the strict sense of the word, and

[31] Canon 2195.

the delinquent, even though unknown, can be punished.[32] Heresy, for example, if it is purely internal, is a grave sin but it is not a crime; if, however, it is in any way manifested externally, it is a crime and, even though the external manifestation has not been observed by any one, the heretic is subject to punishment.

The second qualification mentioned by the canon is that the crime should be grave. The natural law itself demands due proportion between the law violated and the punishment inflicted. The gravity of a crime is to be measured from the importance of the law violated, from the degree of imputability, and from the injury caused[33] and, in determining the proportion between the crime and the punishment, consideration is to be taken of the imputability, scandal and injury, and not only the object and gravity of the law, but the age, knowledge, sex, condition, and state of mind of the delinquent.[34]

Thirdly, the crime, to be punished by censure, should be consummated. This does not mean that an attempted crime cannot be punished by censure for the opposite is indicated in canon 2212 § 4, which states that if an attempted crime is specifically punished by a penalty, it constitutes a true crime, and canons 2351 § 1, and 2407 give practical examples of this. What is meant is that the specific act prohibited should be consummated so that if an attempted crime is prohibited, that attempt, as an attempt, should be consummated.[35]

The fourth qualification is that the crime should be joined with contumacy. Contumacy may be defined as obstinate disregard of the requirements of legitimate authority. It is precisely to overcome this that censures are inflicted, and in this they are differentiated from other ecclesiastical punishments. Contumacy, by the very nature of the case, presupposes knowledge of the requirements of legitimate authority. The knowl-

---

[32] Canon 2242, § 1.
[33] Canon 2196.
[34] Canon 2218.
[35] Canon 2228, Vermeersch-Creusen, III, 420.

edge of censure sufficient to give rise to contumacy, is brought to delinquents by canonical warning, given either *a iure,* or *ab homine,* depending upon whether the censure is *latae* or *ferendae sententiae.* In the case of censures *ferendae sententiae,* a person is contumacious if, disregarding the warning given him as prescribed in canon 2233 § 2, he persists in committing the crime, or fails to repent and properly repair the injury and scandal caused by a crime, already committed.[36] Formerly, in the case of censures *ferendae sententiae,* a threefold warning at determined intervals was required but now a single warning, if disregarded, is sufficient to indicate contumacy.

In the case of censures *latae sententiae,* a delinquent is contumacious by the very fact of transgressing the law or precept to which he knows the punishment is attached.[37] The very fact that the law orders something under penalty of ipso facto censure is, in itself, a general warning, and sufficient to indicate contumacy on the part of the person who disregards it. Since the person must know of the censure threatened by law in order to be contumacious, a censure cannot be inflicted for a past crime, because at the time the person committed the crime he could not know of the censure since it did not exist. But if the crime is permanent, that is if it has a successive tract as, for example, the unlawful detention of Church property, or if it is habitual, the delinquent can be punished by censure as long as he persists in the crime.[38]

A delinquent is considered to have receded from his contumacy when he has sincerely repented of the offense committed and made fitting reparation of the injury caused and the scandal given, or at least seriously promises to do so.[39] When this has taken place absolution cannot be denied by one who has the power to grant it.[40]

[36] Canon 2242, § 2.
[37] Sole, No. 160.
[38] D'Annibale, *Summa Theol. Moralis,* I, 329; Lega, III, 85.
[39] Canon 2242, § 3.
[40] Canon 2248, § 2.

The causes which excuse from censure have particular importance in connection with reserved cases because whatever excuses from the censure does away with the consequent reservation.[41] A punishment supposes imputability and a grave punishment like censure supposes grave imputability. Therefore, not only what excuses from all imputability, but whatever excuses from grave imputability, excuses from any penalty, whether *latae* or *ferendae sententiae,* both in the internal and external forum, if the excusing cause can be established in the latter.[42] Hence, whatever excuses the delinquent from grave sin also excuses from incurring the censure, at least in conscience and before God, and in the external forum also, provided he can establish the existence of the excusing cause there. Positing the external violation of a law, guilt or imputability is presumed in the external forum, until the opposite is proven.[43]

Guilt or imputability is the subjective and formal element of crime. Of the causes which take away or diminish imputability, some directly affect the intellect, others directly affect the will, while others directly affect both the intellect and the will. Ignorance, error and inadvertence directly affect the intellect, force and fear directly affect the will, while insanity and immature age directly affect both the intellect and the will.

Legislation regarding imputability is set forth in two places in the Code. The first is from canon 2199 to canon 2211 where general norms are established especially to aid judges and superiors to measure the degree of imputability. Inasmuch as censures *latae sententiae* are inflicted ipso facto, without the intervention of a judge or a superior, it is only fitting that the Legislator should expressly determine the manner in which imputability is affected and this is done in canon 2229 of the Code.

---

[41] Canon 2246, § 3.
[42] Canon 2218.
[43] Canon 2200, § 2.

The most common cause affecting imputability is ignorance. To understand properly the effect of ignorance upon the incurring of a punishment it will be necessary to explain some divisions of ignorance. Ignorance is the lack of due knowledge of something; it differs from error and inadvertence, yet all three have practically the same effect upon imputability, and consequently, the same rules that apply to ignorance apply, in general, to error and inadvertence.[44] *Ignorance of law* is lack of knowledge of the existence of some law, or of the matter contained in the law; *ignorance of fact* is lack of knowledge of the terminus or object of an action. If, for example, a delinquent knew of the law forbidding the striking of clerics, but did not know that the particular person he struck was a cleric, his ignorance would be ignorance of fact. If a delinquent knows of the law, and also knows some particular fact comes under the law, but does not know the penalty attached to violation of the law, his ignorance is termed *ignorance of penalty.*

Ignorance is further divided into culpable and inculpable ignorance. It is culpable when it can be dispelled by the use of due moral diligence, and the person, suspecting his ignorance, fails to use this diligence. It is inculpable, if the person in no way suspects his ignorance, or, if suspecting it, he uses due moral diligence but is unable to dispel it.

Culpable ignorance is subdivided into affected culpable ignorance and negligent culpable ignorance. Affected culpable ignorance is that which is directly willed and procured, for example, a man who lays aside a book he is reading lest he should learn from it that an action he is committing is sinful. Negligent, culpable ignorance is that which is not directly but only indirectly willed, inasmuch as it results from lack of due diligence in seeking the truth. It is only slightly culpable, if the negligence from which it proceeds is only venially sinful; it is gravely culpable, if it results from a serious neglect of

[44] Canon 2202, § 3.

the use of diligence. It is crass and supinely culpable if it results not merely from grave negligence, but from enormously grave negligence.[45]

The following diagram may aid in clarifying these divisions of ignorance:

- Ignorance
  - Of Law
  - Of Fact
  - Of Punishment
- Ignorance
  - Inculpable
  - Culpable
    - Affected
    - Negligent
      - Slight
      - Grave
      - Crass or Supine

The laws determining the effect of ignorance upon incurring penalties are based upon these divisions of ignorance. Violation of a law is not imputable, if it results from inculpable ignorance, error or inadvertence, whether of law or of fact, and consequently inculpable ignorance excuses from punishments both *latae* and *ferendae sententiae,* in the internal as well as in the external forum. But ignorance merely of penalty does not take away imputability, although it lessens it somewhat and as a general rule, therefore, even inculpable ignorance merely of penalty will not excuse the delinquent; he knowingly violated a law, is objectively and subjectively guilty, and so there is nothing unjust in inflicting a proportionate penalty.[46] Censures, however, are an exception to this rule because, by their very nature, they presuppose knowledge and consequently ignorance merely of censure excuses from incurring it.[47] A second exception to the principle that ignorance merely of the punishment does not excuse from incurring it arises in the case of punishments *latae sententiae,* as will be seen presently. It is to be clearly understood that the principles

[45] Suarez, *De Legibus,* lib. v, cap. 12, No. 14.
S. Alphonsus, VII, 47.
Lega, III, 55.

[46] Canon 2202, § 2; Lega, III, 57.

[47] Canon 2242; Suarez, *De Censuris,* disp. 4, sect 8; Lega, III, 57; Sole, No. 29.

which have been set forth refer to the effect of ignorance of censure, and not to the effect of ignorance of the reservation of the censure. If, however, the superior expressly indicates that the reservation is a punishment the general rules regarding the effect of ignorance upon punishments can be applied to reservation; per se, however, they cannot.

Culpable Ignorance

When ignorance is culpable, it does not take away imputability but it diminishes it in proportion with the degree of the culpability. Hence, venially culpable ignorance excuses from eccleciastical punishments in keeping with the dictum "Parum pro nihilo habetur."

Gravely culpable ignorance does not excuse from grave guilt, though it lessens it somewhat, and consequently a judge or superior may inflict punishment on a delinquent, who committed a crime through gravely, culpable ignorance. However, in punishments *latae sententiae,* since the penalty is not directly inflicted through the medium of a judge or a superior, special rules are established in canon 2229 concerning the effect of ignorance upon punishments *latae sententiae.*

Affected ignorance, whether of law or of penalty, does not excuse from any punishment *latae sententiae,* not even if the words of the law demand full and complete deliberation and consent. Before the Code this was held as an opinion by some, but denied by others.[48] The Code settles the question, by expressly stating that even though the wording of the law does demand full imputability, affected ignorance will not excuse from the punishment. While affected ignorance is not psychologically the same as full knowledge, it is morally equivalent to it, and so it is quite proper that it should not excuse from punishment.[49]

If the law contains such words as "praesumpserit", "ausus

---

[48] Suarez, De Legibus, lib. v, Cap. 12, No. 6; D'Annibale, I, 312; Salmanticenses X, I, 199; Sanchez 11, 10, 38.

[49] Vermeersch-Creusen, III, 424.

fuerit", "scienter", "studiose", "consulto egerit" or similar words requiring full knowledge and deliberation, any lessening of imputability excuses from punishments, *latae sententiae.*[50] Therefore, even crass or supine ignorance excuses from punishments *latae sententiae,* when the wording of the law indicates that complete and full imputability is required for its violation. If, on the other hand, the law does not indicate this, crass or supine ignorance does not excuse from punishments *latae sententiae.*

Simply grave ignorance of the law or even of the penalty, and even though the law does not contain words similar to those mentioned above, excuses from medicinal, but not from vindictive punishments, *latae sententiae.* Therefore, grave ignorance, provided it is not crass and supine, either of the law or merely of the punishment excuses from all censures *latae sententiae.*

To sum up, briefly, the effect of ignorance upon incurring censures: Inculpable ignorance, or venially culpable ignorance, either of law or of fact or of censure, excuses from incurring the censure; simple gravely culpable ignorance excuses from censures *latae sententiae;* Crass or supine ignorance does not excuse from censures *latae sententiae,* unless the wording of the law indicates that the fullest imputability is necessary for its violation; affected ignorance never excuses. In all these cases, it naturally follows that if the censure is not incurred, the delinquent is not affected by the reservation, if the censure happened to be reserved, and any simple confessor could absolve.

Lack of the use of reason

A second cause excusing from censure, and consequently from its reservation, is lack of the use of reason. Those who actually lack the use of reason are incapable of committing a crime because the basis of imputability is then lacking.[51] Habitually insane, even though they sometimes have lucid inter-

[50] Canon 2229.

[51] Canon 2201, § 1.

vals, are presumed incapable of crime. Intoxication affects the use of reason, and a crime committed as a result of voluntary intoxication, is indeed imputable but not in the same degree as if it were committed by one in full possession of the use of his faculties, unless intoxication was directly sought as a means to commit or excuse a crime. Violation of a law resulting from involuntary intoxication is not imputable if the intoxication takes away entirely the use of reason; if it only partly takes it away, the degree of imputability depends upon the degree of the use of reason unaffected. This same principle can be applied to all similar mental disturbances. A general principle governing the effect of all these forms of mental disorder upon punishments *latae sententiae* is given in canon 2229, § 3—if, notwithstanding the diminished imputability, the action remains mortally sinful, the delinquent is not excused from punishments *latae sententiae* and conversely, if the action is not mortally sinful, he is excused. The delinquent will be affected by the reservation or not accordingly as he incurs the censure or not.

Force and Fear

Physical violence, which completely takes away freedom of action, takes away the basis or foundation of crime.[52] Grave fear, even though relative, as well as necessity and grave inconvenience, generally excuse from a crime, unless the latter involves contempt of faith or of ecclesiastical authority, or gives rise to public, spiritual injury. Even light fear excuses from punishments *latae sententiae* if the law contain words indicating the necessity of complete imputability.

Minor Age

As a general rule, the fact that a delinquent is a minor diminishes the guilt of his crime, and it does so in proportion with the proximity to infancy.[53] Consequently a minor is excused from punishments *latae sententiae* attached to laws which

[52] Canon 2205, § 1.
[53] Canon 2204.

demand complete imputability as specified in canon 2229, § 2, unless it is certain that this full imputability is not affected in the least by the immaturity of the delinquent. Moreover, minors, who have not reached the age of puberty, are excused from all punishments *latae sententiae,* and therefore are not affected by their reservation.[54] A minor, if a male, is presumed to attain the age of puberty at the completion of his fourteenth year, and, if a female, at the completion of her twelfth year.[55] Before the Code, in criminal matters, the age of puberty was considered as the same for males and females, namely, the completion of the fourteenth year.[56] Can this opinion be held after the Code? On strictly juridical grounds, it does not seem that it can because the Code lays down a general principle determining the age of puberty and it does not make an exception to this principle in criminal matters. Vermeersch-Creusen[57] expresses the view that the opinion can still be retained after the Code, and give as a reason the analogy contained in canon 1648, § 3, which allows minors to act personally in spiritual cases and in cases connected with the spiritual, after they have completed the age of fourteen. But this reason is not conclusive since it is not evident that this exception is to be extended to include the age of puberty in the application of the laws governing ecclesiastical punishments.

Multiplication of Censure

Having explained the notion of censure and the causes that excuse from incurring it, there is one other point which requires some explanation before passing on to absolution from censure and its reservation, namely the possibility of a person being bound by several censures, and therefore by several reservations at one and the same time. At first sight it would appear that a person already deprived of spiritual goods by the censure

---

[54] Canon 2230.
[55] Canon 88.
[56] Lega, III, 28.
[57] Vermeersch-Creusen, III, 424.

of excommunication could not possibly suffer further deprivation, and consequently could not incur another censure. Though it is true that censure is a privation, and a privation, in se, does not admit of increase, yet such a privation can be increased in the sense that it can be imposed on multiple titles, and it is possible, therefore, for a delinquent to be bound by more than one censure.[58] As commentators point out, censures are like so many bonds or chains, and just as a person can be bound by many chains, either of a similar or different character, so a delinquent can be bound by more than one censure of the same or different species and just as one chain can be removed without removing others, so one censure can be removed without removing others, and the entire privation remains because of the remaining title or titles.[59]

Censures are multiplied as often as diverse crimes, punished by censure, are committed by a single act or by distinct actions,[60] and as often as the same crime is repeated so as to constitute several distinct crimes, or as often as a crime is committed to which distinct censures have been attached by different superiors. Finally, censures *ab homine* are multiplied as often as several precepts or several sentences, or different parts of the same precept or sentence, inflict distinct censures.

[58] Canon 2244; Vermeersch-Creusen, III, 440.
[59] Canon 2249; Lega III, 102.
[60] Canon 2244.

3. *Absolution from Censure*

In setting forth the legislation on absolution from censure and its reservation, the arrangement of the matter of the following chapters will differ somewhat from the order followed by the Code from canon 2245 to canon 2254. An examination of these canons reveals that the first three refer to reservation of censure, the next four to absolution from censure, in general, and the final three to absolution from reserved censures. Inasmuch as a proper understanding of reservation of the power to absolve presupposes knowledge of the laws governing absolution from censure in general, it will, perhaps, be more logical to treat the latter first, and then group together the canons referring to reservation of censure.

When a censure has once been contracted, it can be removed only by legitimate absolution.[1] A censure actually incurred continues to bind after the death of the superior who inflicted it because a positive disposition of law renders it binding until removed by absolution. Nor are the effects of censure fully and completely taken away by the death of the censured delinquent because a censure not only affects the delinquent but it also indirectly affects the faithful in general by imposing upon them the obligation of refraining from certain actions in reference to the delinquent; an example of this is furnished by canon 1240, § 1 No. 2 which declares that after a condemnatory or declaratory sentence persons who are excommunicated or interdicted cannot be granted Christian burial.[2]

A censure is not ipso facto removed by the repentance and satisfaction of the delinquent; these constitute the reason why the superior should absolve, but do not of themselves remove the censure. Censures differ from vindictive punishments in

[1] Canon 2248, § 1.
[2] Wernz, VI, 173; Cappello, *De Censuris*, No. 28.

the manner of their removal—censures are removed by absolution, vindictive punishments either cease by the very nature of the case when the punishment is fulfilled, or they are removed by dispensation, granted by a legitimate superior. As Cardinal Lega points out, the diverse ends of ecclesiastical punishments should be kept in mind, when examining the differences between absolution and dispensation.[3] Censures are medicinal and inflicted precisely to correct the delinquent and consequently, having accomplished this end, they should be removed, so that a censure, by its very nature, tends to absolution. Vindictive punishment, on the contrary, binds the delinquent either perpetually or for a defined time. In the case of censure, absolution is an act of justice, in the case of vindictive punishments, dispensation is an act of charity because vindictive punishments do not demand, but permit dispensation.

One must be careful not to confuse the cessation of a law or precept inflicting censure with the cessation of a censure already incurred as a result of that law or precept. A law or precept inflicting censure can cease as any other law or precept, but this has no effect on a censure already incurred; the latter binds even after the cessation of the law or precept inflicting it and can only be removed by absolution.[4]

To absolve validly from censure the same subjective dispositions are not required in the delinquent as are necessary to absolve validly from sin. For the latter at least supernatural attrition is necessary, but in absolution from censure all that is required is that the delinquent has receded from his contumacy and repaired, or at least promises to repair, the injury and scandal caused by his crime, and even though this disposition is prompted by purely natural motives the absolution from censure would be valid. Suppose the delinquent has not receded from his contumacy but is nevertheless granted absolution, would the absolution be valid? A distinction is to be made between ordinary power and delegated power to absolve. If

[3] Lega, III, 103.
[4] Canon 2226, § 3.

the absolution is granted by one with ordinary power to absolve, it would be unlawful but valid because there is nothing from the nature of the case, or positive law, that renders it invalid. But if granted by one having delegated power to absolve, the absolution would be invalid, if the proper disposition of the delinquent was a "conditio sine qua non" of the delegation of power.[5]

Since the same conditions are not necessary to absolve validly from censure as to absolve validly from sin, it is quite possible to absolve from censure without absolving from the connected sin. One sin cannot be forgiven independently of others, because forgiveness of sin is effected by the infusion of Sanctifying Grace, which will not take place as long as a single mortal sin remains on the soul. But it is possible to absolve from one censure without absolving from others, which may bind the delinquent, so that it is not necessary to absolve all in order to absolve from one. If, for example, the delinquent has fulfilled all the requisites for the lawful absolution of one censure, but has not completely repaired the scandal caused by a crime which has given rise to a second censure, the Superior can absolve from the first without absolving the second censure.[6]

Absolution from censure is always direct, and consequently the person seeking absolution should indicate all the censures he has incurred, otherwise the absolution will be valid only for the cases indicated. If, however, the delinquent, in good faith, fails to mention some censures, and the superior grants absolution in general terms, all the censures would be directly absolved except those reserved *specialissimo modo* to the Holy See.[7] So, per se, absolution from censure is only valid for cases expressly mentioned but, by a special provision of law, it is valid also for censures which the person inculpably fails to mention, provided the absolution is granted by a general form, and provided the censure is not reserved *specialissimo modo* to

[5] Wernz, VI, 176.
[6] Canon 2249.
[7] Canon 2249, § 2, Sole, No. 181.

the Holy See. A censure deliberately concealed is not absolved even if absolution is granted in general terms.

In determining the relation between a censure and the connected sin, a distinction must be made between those censures which impede the reception of the sacraments and those which do not. There are three species of censure—excommunication, suspension and interdict. Of these three species, excommunication and personal interdict impede the lawful reception of the Sacraments,[8] while suspension and local interdict do not carry with them this canonical effect. Therefore, a penitent, who is suspended, if otherwise properly disposed, can be absolved lawfully from sin but one who is excommunicated or personally interdicted can not be absolved lawfully from sin unless first absolved from the censure.[9] The effect which reservation of the censure has upon the connected sin will be pointed out later.

By Divine institution, the Church exercises her authority in two fora, the internal and the external.[10] The internal forum is that in which matters of conscience are regulated. It is directly concerned with Christians as individuals and only indirectly with the faithful considered as a corporate whole, in so far as the welfare of the corporate body is indirectly promoted by the welfare of the individual. The authority of the Church in the external forum is exercised directly upon matters which pertain to the public corporate good of the whole Christian society. The internal forum is divided into the sacramental and extra-sacramental forum. Matters of conscience connected with the Sacrament of Penance pertain to the internal, sacramental forum; other matters of conscience which can be expedited outside of sacramental confession pertain to the internal, extra-sacramental forum.[11]

A censure is essentially a bond of the external forum, imposed by the external and social coercive power of the Church

[8] Canons 2260, § 1, and 2275, § 2.
[9] Canon 2250, § 1 and § 2.
[10] Canon 209.
[11] D'Annibale, I, 25.

and consequently, per se, a censure should be absolved in the external forum, yet the Church permits absolution to be given in the internal forum, whether sacramental or extra-sacramental,[12] but the effects of absolution granted in the internal forum are not as complete as when the absolution is granted in the external forum. When the absolution is granted in the external forum it produces its effects in both fora, that is the bond of censure is removed in the eyes of the Church as well as in conscience and before God; but when granted in the internal forum, while its effects are fully removed in conscience and before God, yet the principle "nihil est nisi quod apparet" applies in the external forum, and consequently the censure can be urged in the external forum by a Superior unless the obtaining of absolution in the internal forum can be proved or lawfully presumed.[13] A delinquent, absolved in the internal forum from an occult censure, can act as one truly absolved because no scandal would be caused, but if the censure is notorious or public, a person absolved only in the internal forum would have to refrain from actions that would give rise to scandal, though he can act occultly against the prohibitions of the censure which urge in the external forum.[14]

No form of absolution is so prescribed that the validity of the absolution is dependent upon its use. As far as validity is concerned, it is sufficient that the grant of absolution is manifested by some sensible sign indicating the intention of a competent superior to grant absolution. In the sacramental forum, the form of absolution from censure precedes the form of absolution from sin contained in the Ritual; in the non-sacramental forum, whether internal or external it is also best to use the form prescribed in the Ritual, especially in absolving from excommunication.[15] In the Roman Ritual this form is found under chapter 2 of title III: "Absolutionis forma", and also in

[12] Canon 2239, § 1.
[13] Canon 2251.
[14] Chelodi, No. 34.
[15] Canon 2251; Wernz, VI, 186.

chapter 3: "De absolutione ab excommunicatione in foro exteriori", and again in chapter V: "De modo absolvendi a suspensione vel ab interdicto extra vel intra sacramentalem confessionem." In the Roman Pontifical, the form is contained under the titles: "Ordo suspensionis, reconciliationis, etc." and "Ordo Excommunicandi et absolvendi." If the censure was inflicted through a written document it is expedient that its absolution should also be granted in writing.[16]

It is not necessary that the delinquent be present when absolution from censure is granted. If the delinquent is not present it is certain that a competent superior can grant absolution through the medium of a letter. By the nature of the case, the presence of the delinquent is necessary when absolution is granted in the internal, sacramental forum, but this is not true of the internal, extra-sacramental forum, and consequently there is no reason why absolution granted in the latter forum to an absent delinquent would be invalid.[17]

Absolution may be granted conditionally and the conditions may refer to the present, past or future.[18] When granted dependent upon a condition referring to the present or past, the absolution will produce its effects immediately or not, accordingly as the condition is verified or not. If given on a condition referring to the future, the effect of the absolution will be suspended until such time as the condition is verified and then, since the presence of the delinquent is not necessary when absolution is granted, the absolution produces its effect.

A censure, once absolved, does not revive but a competent superior, when granting absolution, can impose something to be done under penalty of reincidence, that is, if the delinquent fails to carry out the mandate of the superior, he, ipso facto, incurs a new censure of the same kind as the one from which he was absolved.[19] In this case the person is really absolved

[16] Canon 2239, § 2.
[17] Canon 2239, § 1.
[18] D'Annibale, I, 354.
[19] Canon 2248, § 3.

from the first censure and it does not revive and the censure incurred is an altogether new one, though of exactly the same kind as the one absolved.

4. *Reservation of Censure and Its Consequences*

The notion and effect of reservation have already been described in the first chapter of this treatise, but they were considered in a generic sense and attention was primarily given to stress the notion of reservation and its effects in connection with sins reserved *ratione sui.* Because the laws regulating the absolution from reserved sins and absolution from reserved censures differ essentially, it is necessary to separate the treatment of both, but despite these essentially different norms regulating their absolution, reservation of sin and reservation of censure have the same nature and end. Though it necessitates some repetition, it will be appropriate to recall in a summary way the notion of reservation and specifically apply it to censure in order to clarify points which might otherwise be obscure.

Reservation has been defined as: "Avocatio quorundum peccatorum et censurarum ad superioris iudicium, a legitimo superiore facta, inferioribus absolvendi potestatem limitando." Hence reservation of censure is a limitation of the power to absolve from censure. Two elements enter into the power to absolve from sin—one the power of orders, the other the power of jurisdiction. But in absolution from censure, there is, per se, only one element, that of jurisdiction. The power of orders to absolve from sin arises from ordination itself but cannot be validly exercised without the power of jurisdiction, which is obtained from the concession of a competent superior. In absolution from censure, the entire power depends upon the concession of a competent superior. Therefore, reservation of the power to absolve from sin is a positive limitation inasmuch as it limits an inchoate power already present in virtue of ordination. Reservation of the power to absolve from censure is rather a negative limitation, inasmuch as the superior does not grant power which is in no way already present in the subject.[20]

[20] Sole, No. 170; D'Annibale, II, 338, note 16.

By restricting the power to absolve from a censure, the superior forces the delinquent to come to him, or to the one to whom he has reserved the censure, in order to obtain absolution. Reservation of censure, therefore, has the same effect and purpose as reservation of sin—it limits an inferior's jurisdiction and forces the delinquent to seek absolution from one who is specially qualified to handle the case in the best interests of ecclesiastical discipline. Censure itself is a punishment; reservation of the censure, per se, is not a punishment but a disciplinary measure. It is evident, from the very nature of censure, that the primary purpose of reservation is not to render its absolution more difficult, because once the delinquent has receded from his contumacy he has a right to absolution and reservation of the censure does not take away this right. But the proper regulation of ecclesiastical discipline urges that more serious crimes should receive the special consideration of competent superiors. The crime committed may be of such character as to warrant the infliction of a vindictive punishment, or other special remedies,[21] and the ordinary confessor has not the power to inflict vindictive punishments nor is he as qualified as the superior to prescribe the best remedies, and through reservation the Superior provides for all of these elements. Per se, then, reservation of censure is not a punishment; it is connected with a punishment, and may be the means of bringing a delinquent before a superior for further punishment, but in itself it is not a punishment unless a superior expressly makes it such as did Benedict XIV in the reservation attached to false denunciation.[22]

If it is expressly indicated that reservation is a punishment, all the laws referring to punishment will apply to it, otherwise they do not. We have already described the effect of ignorance and indicated how it excuses from censure, but it is to be borne in mind that these laws refer to ignorance of censure and other

[21] Canon 2248, § 2.

[22] Benedict XIV, const. *Sacramentum Poenitentiae;* Doc. V in Code.

ecclesiastical punishments and not to reservation when it is not a punishment. If it is not expressly indicated that reservation is a punishment, ignorance merely of the reservation will not excuse from it; ignorance of the censure will excuse from it and consequently from its reservation, but ignorance only of the reservation will not because, when used as a disciplinary measure, the delinquent's ignorance of the fact that absolution from the censure requires, in the judgment of ecclesiastical superiors, specially expert consideration does not take away that need.

In accordance with the principle "odiosa sunt restringenda," reservation of censure is to be interpreted strictly, and consequently it does not bind in doubt of law or of fact.[23] As long as there is a positive doubt as to whether the penitent is affected by the reservation, any confessor may lawfully and validly absolve, and the absolution would be direct even though it became certain later that the reservation applied.[24]

The division of reserved censures is based upon the distinction between censures, *ab homine and a iure.* It will be recalled that a censure *a iure* is one which is determined in the law itself, whether *latae* or *ferendae;* a censure *ab homine* is one which is inflicted by a particular precept or by a condemnatory sentence, and that a censure *ferendae sententiae,* added to a law is only *a iure* before a condemnatory sentence but after such sentence it is both *a iure* and *ab homine,* though it is considered as *ab homine.*[25]

All censures *ab homine* are reserved to the one who inflicted the censure, or gave the sentence, or to the competent superior, successor, or delegate of these.[26] The wording of the canon which states this principle is somewhat misleading. It reads: "Censura 'ab homine' est reservata ei qui censuram inflixit aut sententiam tulit, eiusve Superiori competenti, vel successori aut

[23] Canons 2246, §2 and 2245, § 4.
[24] Canon 209.
[25] Canon 2217, § 1, No. 3.
[26] Canon 2245, § 2.

delegato." The phrase "aut sententiam tulit" would incline one to think that a censure inflicted by a condemnatory sentence is reserved to the judge, who issued the sentence. But it is not true that such a censure is reserved to the judge, merely in his capacity as judge. A judge, merely as a judge, does not establish a penalty when he issues a condemnatory sentence, but only applies a penalty, already established by a competent superior. One who possesses only judicial power cannot establish a penalty; he can only apply, in accordance with the norms of law, penalties already established, and, having applied them, he cannot absolve or dispense from them.[27] Therefore, the phrase "aut sententiam tulit" in canon 2245 does not mean that censure *ab homine* is reserved to a judge, merely as a judge; it means that a censure *ab homine* is reserved to the superior who established it and who exercised his judicial power, either per se vel per alios, in inflicting it.[28] As a consequence of the ambiguity of this first phrase, the words "eiusve Superiore competenti" are also misleading. This second phrase does not mean that a censure *ab homine,* imposed by the tribunal of first instance, is reserved to, or can be absolved by, the tribunal of second instance. It is true a delinquent, convicted in the first instance, may appeal *in devolutivo* against the sentence of censure, to the tribunal of second instance.[29] The tribunal of second instance, after retrying the case, may reverse the decision given in the first and find the defendant not guilty. But by so doing the tribunal of second instance does not absolve from the censure, it merely retries the case and decides that the censure is not to be applied. Consequently, "eiusve Superiori competenti" in canon 2245 means the jurisdictional superior of the one who established the censure. For this reason a Metropolitan cannot absolve from a censure *ab homine* imposed by one of the Ordinaries of his Province except in the case mentioned in canon 274, No. 5.

[27] Canons 2220 and 2236, § 3.
[28] Canon 1572, § 1; Sole, No. 147.
[29] Canon 2243.

Strangely, after stating that a censure *ab homine* is reserved, paragraph 4 of canon 2245 states "Censura latae sententiae non est reservata, nisi in lege vel precepto, id expresse dicatur." A censure *ab homine* may also be *latae sententiae,* and consequently there appears to be a contradiction between Nos. 1 and 4 of canon 2245—the former states that a censure *ab homine* is reserved, the latter states that if it is *latae sententiae* it is not reserved unless expressly stated. Some authors conclude that the law has been changed and that now a censure *latae sententiae,* whether *a iure* or *ab homine,* is not reserved unless expressly stated.[80] But it appears that in canon 2245 No. 4 the Code means censures *a iure* only. This is indicated by the context of canon 2245, by canon 2217 and by canon 2253, which is a parallel canon, to be taken in conjunction with canon 2245, and which sets up a distinction in its second and third parts between censures *ab homine,* and censures *a iure* and indicates that all of the former are reserved. Moreover, it was the universal teaching of canonists before the Code, that all censures *ab homine,* whether *latae sententiae* or *ferendae sententiae,* were reserved. These arguments indicate so strongly that No. 4 of canon 2245 applies only to censures *a iure,* that there are scarcely sufficient grounds for a doubt of law on this point. The conclusion is, therefore, that all censures *ab homine* are reserved either to the one who established the censure or to his competent superior, successor or delegate.

Censures *a iure* are not reserved unless express mention of the reservation is made in the law itself. Censures *a iure* may be established either by the Holy See or by Ordinaries inferior to the Holy See. Censures reserved *a iure* by the Holy See are reserved either to the Holy See or to inferior Ordinaries. Those reserved to the Holy See are reserved either "simpliciter," or "speciali modo," or "specialissimo modo." The basis of this last division is not the nature of the reservation, because all

[80] Sole, No. 173.

three are reserved to the Holy See, but it designates the kind of faculties needed to absolve from such reservations.[31]

The following diagram indicates the various divisions of reserved censures:

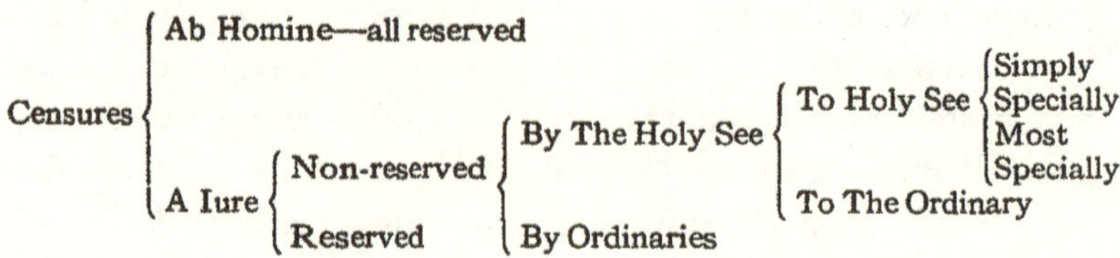

It has been pointed out, in a previous chapter, that a censure which impedes the reception of the sacraments, impedes the licit absolution from the connected sin. Suppose the censure is one which not only impedes the reception of the sacraments but is also reserved, what is its effect on absolution from the connected sin? In this case the sin to which the reserved censure is connected is also reserved and[32] consequently a reserved censure which impedes the reception of the sacraments, not only impedes the licit, but also the valid absolution of the sin to which it is attached. In other words, there is really a twofold reservation in this case, one of the censure, the other of the sin; the censure is directly reserved, the sin to which it is attached is indirectly reserved and is therefore said to be reserved *ratione censurae,* in contradiction to a sin which is directly reserved *ratione sui.*

If any person is excused for any reason from incurring a censure that is reserved, the sin to which it is attached is not reserved, or, if the censure is incurred, when the delinquent is absolved from it, the reservation of the connected sin ceases.[33] This follows logically from the nature of the reservation of the connected sin—since it is reserved *ratione censurae,* the reservation is dependent on the censure, so that if the censure is not incurred, or, having been incurred, if absolution has removed

[31] Canon 2253, No. 3.
[32] Canon 2246.
[33] E. g., Canon 2314, § 2.

it, the sin to which it is attached is not reserved. Because of this, it is absolutely essential, when dealing with reserved cases, to know the various causes which excuse from incurring censure, for if the delinquent is excused for any reason, whether it be ignorance or grave fear or lack of age, or any of the other causes, discussed in a previous chapter, the connected sin is not reserved. This, however, only applies when the connected sin is reserved merely *ratione censurae.* If the superior directly reserves the censure, and also directly reserves the connected sin, the connected sin is then reserved on a twofold title—one reservation is indirect as a result of the reservation of the censure, the other reservation is direct as a result of the direct reservation of the sin itself. In all, there is a threefold reservation in this case; the first is a direct reservation of the censure, and this gives rise to the second, which is the indirect reservation of the connected sin, and the third is the direct reservation of the sin itself. Therefore, when a superior directly reserves a censure, which impedes the reception of the Sacraments, and also directly reserves the connected sin, if the delinquent is excused for any reason from incurring the censure, or if he is absolved from the censure after incurring it, the indirect reservation of the sin resulting from the reservation of the censure no longer holds, nevertheless the connected sin remains reserved *ratione sui* so that a simple confessor cannot absolve from it despite the cessation of the censure. An example of such reservation is found in the Code in the case of the crime of false accusation of an innocent confessor of solicitation. This crime is punished by excommunication, reserved "speciali modo" to the Holy See,[34] consequently the connected sin is reserved *ratione censurae* on this score; but the sin is also directly reserved *ratione sui* to the Holy See[35] so that the sin remains reserved to the Holy See, even though the person is absolved from the censure or excused from incurring it.

[34] Canon 2363.
[35] Canon 894.

In reserved cases a confessor should first determine, whether there is question of a reserved censure or of a sin reserved *ratione sui* or of both. Former chapters have indicated what the confessor can do in cases of sins reserved *ratione sui.* If there is question of a reserved censure, the confessor should next determine whether or not the censure is one which impedes the reception of the Sacraments, that is whether it is a reserved excommunication or personal interdict. If it is a censure of this kind, he should next verify whether or not the censure has really been incurred by questioning the penitent concerning his knowledge of the punishment of censure at the time he committed the crime, whether or not he committed the crime under the influence of grave fear or drunkenness, etc. If this questioning establishes the fact that the censure has really been incurred, the confessor, in ordinary cases, cannot absolve from either the reserved censure or the connected sin. In a later chapter it will be explained what a simple confessor can do, in urgent cases and in danger of death.

5. *The Quality of Reserved Censures*

In its legislation on sins reserved *ratione sui,* the Code gives a detailed description of the kind of sins, which may be reserved and also determines the number of sins an Ordinary may reserve as well as the formalities he should observe, when establishing such reservation. In its legislation on reserved censures, the Code likewise prescribes in a negative and positive way, what kind of censures may be reserved, but it does not determine a numerical limitation or establish formalities to be observed by Ordinaries, when making reservations of censure. The opinion that the numerical restriction of reserved cases, contained in canon 897 applies only to sins reserved *ratione sui,* and not to reserved censures, has already been stated as well as the reasons upon which it is based and so it will be sufficient here merely to refer to a confirming analogy in the Code. The Code mentions only one sin reserved *ratione sui* to the Holy

See while it contains a large number of reserved censures. It is to be expected, because of the very nature of censure, that the Code should not specifically determine the number of reserved censures an Ordinary may establish or prescribe formalities to be observed in the making of reservations of censure. Reservation of sins *ratione sui* is always general and is effected either by law or a general precept; reservation of censure, on the other hand, is frequently particular, e.g., censures *ab homine.* Due to the more general character of reservation of sin *ratione sui,* it is to be expected that the Code should prescribe formalities to be observed by Ordinaries when establishing this kind of reservation and not do so in the case of reservation of censure. Moreover, censure is a punishment and sufficient formalities are prescribed concerning the establishment and infliction of punishment in general, and censures in particular, to render it unnecessary to establish further safeguards for the reservation of such censures, especially in view of the fact that reservation is ipso facto a necessary consequence of censures *ab homine.*

In determining, in a positive way, the kind of censures which may be reserved the Code is not as specific as it is in its corresponding legislation on sins reserved *ratione sui.* It simply states, in general terms, that a censure should not be reserved unless the special gravity of the crime, and the necessity of better safeguarding ecclesiastical discipline and of correcting the faithful, warrant such reservation.[36] The norms given by the Code to aid Ordinaries in judging whether or not a censure should be reserved are:

1—The gravity of the crime—The very fact that a crime is punished by censure indicates that the crime is grave both objectively and subjectively, and consequently when canon 2246 states that a censure should not be reserved "nisi attenta peculiari gravitate delictorum" the implication is that the crime should not be merely ordinarily grave, but unusually grave, if

[36] Canon 2246.

the censure is to be reserved, because, if merely ordinary gravity justified reservation, every censure should be reserved on this score. 2—The second norm suggested by the Code, to indicate whether reservation of censure is opportune, is "necessitate aptius providendi disciplinae ecclesiasticae." Absolution from censure should not be reserved, that is the case should not be called to the tribunal of the superiors, unless this step is necessary or useful to safeguard ecclesiastical discipline. If the crime is one which does not present any special difficulties, if there is no special problem involved in overcoming and preventing it, if it is a crime which any prudent confessor can handle in the best interests of ecclesiastical discipline, there is no need to reserve the censure. But if the crime is so deeply rooted and so widely spread that it threatens to break down ecclesiastical discipline unless the crime and the criminals are given special consideration, the superior should then reserve the censure and handle the case personally because of his special qualifications, based upon his broader realization of the exact conditions throughout the limits of his diocese and on his prudent judgment of the remedies best suited to meet these conditions. This confirms the opinion that, per se, the primary purpose of reservation, whether of sin or of censure, is disciplinary. A consequence of this norm is that the superior should not be satisfied with merely granting faculties to absolve from a reserved censure, when sought by a confessor in a particular case, but he should suggest the advice and the remedies to be given by the confessor to the delinquent. 3—The third norm, suggested by the Code to indicate the expediency of reservation of censure is "necessitate aptius . . . medendi conscientiis fidelium." This again implies that reservation is a means, not of punishment, but of benefiting the delinquent and of restoring him to friendship with God and communion with the faithful.

When a censure has been reserved by the Holy See, an Ordinary cannot inflict another reserved censure against the same crime.[37] A similar, though more extensive prohibition, is made in canon 898, which warns all Ordinaries to refrain from reserving to themselves cases which have already been reserved by the Holy See, and also to refrain, as a general rule, from reserving censures, imposed by common law, even though not reserved. The question arises suppose a reserved censure is imposed by common law against the same crime against which an Ordinary has already established a reserved censure? In this case, because of the above prohibition against double reservation, the general reservation implicitly does away with the particular reservation so that a delinquent would be affected by only one reservation, that of general law.

6. *Territorial Effect Upon the Binding Force of Reservation of Censure*

A comparison between canon 2247, § 2 and canon 900, No. 3, shows that the former establishes the same principle concerning reservation of censure that the latter establishes for reservation of sin; by virtue of canon 900, No. 3, all reservation of sin ceases outside the territory of the reserver; by virtue of canon 2247, § 2, reservation of censure does not exercise its effect outside the territory of the reserver.

The territorial effect upon the binding force of reservation of censure depends upon whether the reservation arises from a censure *a iure* or *ab homine*. If the censure is *a iure*, and imposed by common law, it binds everywhere, because the common law embraces all territory and, consequently, wherever the delinquent goes he is affected by the reservation of the censure. If, for example, a censure is reserved by common law to the Ordinary, the reservation does not cease if the delinquent goes from his own to another diocese because the censure is still reserved to the Ordinary of the diocese to which he goes. A censure *a iure,* therefore, reserved by common law, exerts its force everywhere, taking "everywhere" in a relative sense,

[37] Canon 2247, § 1.

since, per se, the Code refers only to the Latin Church.[38] However there are some censures, contained in the Code, which affect the Orientals as well as the Latins. The Congregation of the Holy Office declared that the Constitution against solicitation applied to the Orientals[39] and a similar declaration was made by Benedict XIV, in the Constitution "Etsi pastoralis."[40] The Congregation for the Propagation of the Faith decided that Orientals "subiici omnibus censuris ab Apostolica Sede latis in materia dogmatum et in Constitutionibus in quibus implicite de iis deponitur, nempe ubi materia ipsa demonstrat eos comprehendi, quatenus non de lege mere ecclesiastica agitur, sed ius naturale et divinum declaratur." The same letter states: "illos fideles subiici nominatim nedum censuris, sed etiam Apostolicis reservationibus latis in Const. Benedicti XIV 'Sacramentum Poenitentiae,' et in Constitutionibus contra sectae massonicae aliisque similibus addictos."[41] Interpreting canon I in the light of these decisions, it is evident that the reserved censures contained in canons 2314, 2317, 2335 and 2368 affect Orientals as well as Latins and consequently a delinquent belonging to the Latin Church could not be absolved from these censures even if he went to a simple confessor of an Oriental rite.

A reservation, *a iure,* of censure established by the law of an Ordinary inferior to the Pope, does not exercise its force outside the territorial boundaries of the reserver, even though the delinquent leaves the territory for the sole purpose of obtaining absolution.[42] Yet this principle has been limited somewhat by a response of the Pontifical Commission for Interpreting the Code.[43] Asked: "Utrum ad normam canonis 893, § 1 and § 2, peregrinus teneatur reservationibus loci in

[38] Canon 1.
[39] S. C. S. Off., 13 Jun. 1710; Collectanea I, 279.
[40] Benedict XIV, const. *Etsi Pastoralis,* 26 May 1742, par. IX, No. V; Collectanea I, 338.
[41] S. C. de Prop. Fide, litt. encyl., 6 Aug. 1885; Collectanea II, 1640.
[42] Canon 2247, § 2.
[43] Pont. Com. ad CC. auth. interpret., 24 Nov. 1920; AAS. XII, 575.

quo degit?" the Commission answered: "Affirmative." Now canon 893, § 1 and § 2, refers to reservation both of sin and censure and consequently the principle that reservation ceases outside of the territory of the reserver is valid only when the delinquent goes to a territory where the censure is not reserved. If he goes to a territory where the censure is reserved, he is affected by the reservation. This response of the Commission is more difficult to understand in connection with reserved censures than it is in connection with reserved sins. It would be clear, even though the Commission had not given this official interpretation, that a delinquent, who committed a sin reserved in his own diocese and then went to another diocese where the sin was also reserved, could not be absolved by a simple confessor of this second diocese, because this follows logically from the principles governing jurisdiction—the confessor to whom he goes in the extern diocese has received his jurisdiction to absolve from sin from the Ordinary of that extern diocese; and this Ordinary has not given jurisdiction to absolve from the sin which the peregrinus has committed, therefore the confessor cannot absolve the peregrinus. But the conclusion does not follow as logically as this in the case of reserved censures because the source of the jurisdiction of the confessor of the extern diocese to absolve from a censure inflicted by the ordinary of another diocese, is not his own Ordinary but common law. Canon 2253, No. 1, states that in the sacramental forum any confessor can absolve from a non-reserved censure. This is the source of a confessor's jurisdiction to absolve from a non-reserved censure inflicted *a iure* by another ordinary. Now since common law is the source of his jurisdiction to absolve from these censures, and since the principle is established by common law that outside the territory of the reserver reservation of censure does not exercise its effect, it should follow that if a delinquent commits a crime and is punished by a censure *a iure* reserved by his own Ordinary, and then goes to another diocese, he could be absolved from this censure by a simple confessor of this second diocese because, according to canon

2247, § 2, the reservation of the censure ceased when the delinquent left the territory of his own Ordinary, and, according to canon 2253, No. 1, any confessor can absolve from a non-reserved censure. But the response, given by the Commission, clearly indicates that peregrini are bound by the reservations both of sins and of censures in force in the place where they are staying, and consequently canon 2247, § 2, must be modified and interpreted to mean that reservation of censure, in a particular territory, does not exercise its effects outside the limits of that territory, but if the delinquent goes to a territory where the same censure is also reserved, he is affected by the reservation in force in this place.

A censure *ab homine* is reserved everywhere and consequently territorial boundaries play no part in effecting the cessation of reservation *ab homine*.[44]

To sum up these principles: A censure reserved *a iure* by common law, binds wherever the law applies; reservation of censures *ab homine* exercises its effect everywhere; reservation of a censure *a iure* established for a particular territory does not exercise its force outside that territory, but if the delinquent goes to a territory where the same censure is also reserved he is affected by this reservation.

[44] Canon 2247, § 2.

7. *Absolution From Reserved Censures*

A. *Absolution From Reserved Censures In Ordinary Cases*

A censure, *ab homine,* is reserved to him who inflicted the censure or issued the sentence, or to his competent superior, successor or delegate. Consequently, absolution from a censure *ab homine* can only be granted by these.[1] Attention has already been called to the fact that "aut sententiam tulit, eiusve Superiori competenti" refers to one with legislative as well as judicial power, and the jurisdictional superior of the one endowed with such power; it does not refer to a judge, as a judge, or to the tribunal of second instance. Hence those who can absolve from censure *ab homine,* in ordinary cases, are the superior who established the censure, or his jurisdictional superior, or the successors or delegates of these. They can grant absolution even though the delinquent has left their territory and gone to another territory.

Absolution from censures reserved *a iure,* can be granted, in ordinary cases, only by the one who established the censure or to whom it is reserved or by the successors, jurisdictional superiors or delegates of these.[2] Wherefore, from a censure reserved by common law to an Ordinary, any ordinary can absolve his subjects and Local Ordinaries can also absolve peregrini within the limits of their territory; from a censure reserved to the Holy See, the Holy See and those to whom the Holy See grants such power, can absolve. This power is called general, if granted for censures reserved simply to the Holy See, special, if given for censures reserved in a special way to the Holy See, and most special, if granted for censures reserved most specially to the Holy See.

[1] Canon 2253, No. 2.
[2] Canon 2253, No. 3.

The Pope can absolve from all censures no matter how reserved, and he can exercise this power personally or through his delegate. Cardinals enjoy the privilege of hearing confessions everywhere, and of absolving from all sins and censures, even reserved, those only excepted which are reserved most specially to the Holy See and those annexed to revelations of secrets of the Holy Office. A Cardinal also has the privilege of choosing a priest to hear his confession and those of his household, and this priest, if he lacks jurisdiction, obtains it ipso iure, to absolve from sins and censures, even reserved, except the two classes of reservations mentioned above.[3]

In occult cases, Ordinaries are given power ipso iure to absolve from censures reserved simply to the Holy See.[4] They can exercise this power personally or through a delegate, and in either the sacramental or extra-sacramental forum.[5] All possess this power who are included under the name of Ordinary, that is Residential Bishops, Abbots or Prelate nullius and their Vicars General, Administrators, Vicars and Prefects Apostolic, and the greater Superiors of exempt, clerical religious.[6]

Every Bishop, whether residential or titular, has the privilege of selecting a confessor for himself and the members of his household and, as in the case of Cardinals, this priest receives, ipso iure, jurisdiction to absolve even from cases reserved by the Local Ordinary or by the Holy See, with the exception of censures reserved most specially to the Holy See and those annexed to revelation of secrets of the Holy Office.[7]

If a Suffragan Bishop fails to make the prescribed diocesan visitation, the Metropolitan of the Province can enter the territory of the former and make the diocesan visitation, after

[3] Canon 239, § 1, Nos. 1 and 2.
[4] Canon 2237, § 2.
[5] Canon 202, § 3.
[6] Canon 198.
[7] Canon 349.

receiving approval of the cause from the Holy See. During this visitation, the Metropolitan can hear confessions in the territory of the Suffragan and can absolve from cases, whether of sin or of censure, reserved by the Bishop.[8]

Any priest making a sea voyage, who has been approved to hear confessions either by his own Ordinary or by the Ordinary of the port from which he set sail or by the Ordinary of any of the ports which the ship touches in the course of the journey can, throughout the duration of the voyage, hear the confessions of his fellow voyagers; moreover, as often as the ship puts into port in the course of the journey, a priest, approved in any way mentioned above, can hear the confessions of those who for any reason come aboard the ship, and he can also hear the confessions of those who request it when he goes ashore, and he can absolve these even from sins and censures reserved to the Ordinary of the place.[9]

Besides these powers, given ipso iure, Ordinaries and Prelates may request delegated powers from the Holy See to absolve from reserved cases, and in accordance with the amplitude of the power thus granted, they may absolve from censures reserved to the Holy See. The document, granting this power, should be carefully examined to determine whether it is general, special or most special power that is granted.

In ordinary cases, a simple confessor has no power over reserved censures unless specially delegated by the Holy See or by his Ordinary. He should, therefore, consult the faculties granted by his Ordinary. In a number of dioceses, the Ordinary grants power to all his confessors to absolve, in occult cases, from censures reserved simply to the Holy See; in other words, the Ordinary delegates the power he himself receives from common law. The following chapters will describe the power which a confessor receives, ipso iure, to absolve from reserved censures in urgent cases and in danger of death.

[8] Canon 274, No. 5.

[9] Canon 883.

If a confessor, who does not know that a censure is reserved, absolves from the censure and the sin, the absolution from the censure is valid, provided it is not *ab homine* or reserved *specialissimo modo* to the Holy See.[10] The absolution thus given would be valid for all other reserved censures. The law makes no distinction, in this case, between reservation established by the Holy See and those established by inferior Ordinaries and consequently it applies to both of these classes of reserved censures. While this canon states that the absolution from the censure is valid, without mentioning that the absolution from the sin is also valid, there can be no doubt that the absolution from the sin is also valid because once the censure has been absolved validly the sin to which it is connected is no longer reserved.

They, who without proper faculties, presume to absolve from an excommunication *latae sententiae,* reserved *specialissimo* or *speciali modo* to the Holy See, incur ipso facto, an excommunication reserved simply to the Holy See.[11] Because of the word "praesumentes," the fullest imputability is required to incur this penalty and any lessening of guilt, no matter how small, will excuse from it.[12] Notice that the penalty is only incurred in the case of absolution from censures *latae sententiae,* reserved *specialissimo* or *speciali modo* to the Holy See—it would not be incurred if a confessor, without due faculties, presumed to absolve from censure *ab homine,* or from a censure reserved *simpliciter* to the Holy See, or reserved to or by the Ordinary, or from reserved suspension or interdict regardless of how they are reserved.

According to canon 2366, a priest, who, without due faculties, presumes to absolve from reserved sins, is ipso facto suspended from hearing confession. This canon applies to absolution from reserved sins and not to absolution from reserved censures as is indicated by the words "a peccatis

[10] Canon 2247.
[11] Canon 2338, § 1.
[12] Canon 2229, § 2.

reservatis," and also by the fact that the Code has already legislated against those who presume to absolve from reserved censures, in the canon mentioned above.[13]

B. Absolution From Reserved Censures in Urgent Cases

The legislation contained in the Code concerning absolution from reserved censures in urgent cases is based upon the celebrated decree of the Holy Office of June 23d, 1886, and upon the authoritative replies subsequently given to questions concerning it.

In the old law, that is before the year 1886, if a delinquent was prevented by some obstacle from going to a competent superior to receive absolution from a reserved censure, a distinction was made by moral theologians and canonists between an impediment which was perpetual, an impediment which was long, and an impediment which was brief in duration. A perpetual impediment was taken in the wide sense to mean one which was really perpetual or one which would be protracted for a period of five years or more; a long impediment was one which would be protracted beyond a period of six months and a short impediment was one of less than six months' duration.[14]

If a delinquent, bound by a reserved censure, was prevented by a permanent impediment from going to a competent superior for absolution, he could be absolved by his bishop or confessor without being bound by the obligation of recurring later to the competent superior.[15] If the impediment was not permanent, but of long duration, he could also be absolved by his bishop or confessor, but in this case he was bound by the obligation of going to the superior, when the impediment ceased, to receive and fulfill the mandate of the latter. If the impediment was of brief duration, the delinquent could never be directly absolved from the reserved censure except by the Holy See, but if some grave case urged, he could be absolved

---

[13] Vermeersch-Creusen, III, 569.
[14] D'Annibale, I, 349.
[15] D'Annibale, I, 349, note 34.

indirectly from the reserved censure by a confessor. The person was considered to be impeded from going to the Holy See if he could not do so personally, that is he did not have to use another person as a messenger, but the more common opinion was that the impediment was not verified if the delinquent could personally write to the Holy See.[16]

In the year 1886, the Congregation of The Inquisition gave the following response, which was issued by the Congregation of the Holy Office on June 23rd, 1886:[17]

1. Utrum tuto adhuc teneri possit sententia docens ad Episcopum aut ad quemlibet sacerdotem approbatum devolvi absolutionem casuum et censurarum, etiam speciali modo Papae reservatorum, quando poenitens versatur in impossibilitate personaliter adeundi S. Sedem.

2. Quatenus negative: utrum recurrendum sit, saltem per litteras ad Emum Card. Poenitentiarium pro omnibus casibus Papae reservatis nisi Episcopus habeat speciale indultum, praeterquam in articulo mortis, ad obtinendam absolvendi facultatem.

Resp: Ad. 1. Attenta praxi S. Poenitentiariae, praesertim ab edita Constitutione Apostolica sac. mem. Pii PP. IX quae incipit "Apostolicae Sedis," Negative.

Ad. 2. Affirmative; at in casibus vere urgentioribus, in quibus absolutio differri nequeat absque periculo gravis scandali vel infamiae, super quo confessariorum conscientia oneratur, dari posse absolutionem, iniunctis de iure iniungendis, a censuris etiam speciali modo Summo Pontifici reservatis, sub poena tamen reincidentiae in easdem censuras, nisi saltem infra mensem per epistolam et per medium confessarii recurrat ad S. Sedem. Facto verbo cum SSmo. SSmus approbavit.

Authors disputed whether this response referred to those who were impeded by a perpetual impediment or merely to those who were impeded by a long or a brief impediment from going to the Holy See and they also disputed whether the obli-

---

[16] St. Alphonsus, VI, 563.

[17] S. C. S. Off., 23 Jun. 1886; Collect. II, 1658.

gation of recurring under penalty of reincidence applied when absolution was given from a censure reserved *simpliciter modo* to the Holy See. So the following questions were submitted and answered:[18]

1. Utrum responsum ad primum valeat etiam pro casu quando poenitens fuerit perpetuo impeditus personaliter Romam proficisci.

2. Utrum responsi ad secundum clausula "sub poena tamen reincidentiae in easdem censuras etc" referatur solummodo ad absolutionem a censuris et casibus speciali modo S.P. reservatis, an etiam ad absolutionem a censuris simpliciter Papae reservatis.

Ad. 1 Affirmative.

Ad. 2 Negative ad primam partem; affirmative ad secundam partem.

The Decree of 1886, therefore, changed the old opinion that one prevented by a perpetual impediment from seeking absolution from the Holy See could, by that fact alone, be absolved by his Bishop or confessor. All who incurred a censure reserved to the Holy See had to seek absolution from the Holy See, at least by letter. In urgent cases, however, that is if absolution from the censure could not be deferred without danger of grave scandal or infamy, the confessor could grant absolution even from censure reserved *speciali modo* to the Holy See, but in all cases he had to impose upon the penitent, the obligation of recurring, under penalty of reincidence, to the Holy See at least by letter and through the medium of the confessor, within a month after receiving absolution. The reason why no mention is made of censure reserved *specialissimo modo* to the Holy See is that this division of censure did not exist at this time. It was later declared that the absolution given in these urgent cases was direct.[19]

[18] S. C. S. Off., 17 Jun. 1891; Collect. II, 1756.
[19] S. C. S. Off., 19 Aug. 1891; Collect. II, 1764.

A response, given on June 16, 1897,[20] extended urgent cases to include not only those in which absolution could not be deferred without danger of infamy or grave scandal but those also in which it would be difficult for the penitent to remain in grave sin during the time necessary to obtain the faculty to absolve from the reserved censure.

The next difficulty discussed by authors was the case where neither the penitent or the confessor could write to the Holy See, and as a result the following response was given: [21]

1. Utrum decretum S.R. et U. Inquisitionis, datum sub die 23 Iunii 1886, intelligendum sit tantum de iis, qui corporaliter S. Sedem adiri nequeunt; vel etiam de iis, qui ne per litteras quidem per se, neque per confessarium, ad S. Sedem recurrere valent.
2. Et quatenus decretum praedictum extendi debeat etiam ad eos qui ne per litteras quidem ad S. Sedem recurrere valent, quomodo se gerere debeat confessarius.
Resp: Ad. 1 et 2. Quando neque confessarius neque poenitens epistolam ad S. Poenitentiariam mittere possunt, et durum sit poenitenti adire alium confessarium, in hoc casu liceat confessario poenitentem absolvere, etiam a casibus S. Sedi reservatis, absque onere mittendi epistolam.

This response was clarified by a subsequent one given on Sept. 5th, 1900;[22]

An ut onus epistolam mittendi cesset, scribendi impedimentum adstringere debeat confessarium simul et poenitentem; vel sufficiat, sicuti aliqui interpretati sunt, quod poenitens scribendi impar, eidem confessario a quo vi decret, 1886 et 1897 absolutus fuerit, se praesentare nequeat, et ipsi durum sit alium confessarium adire; licet confessarius absolvens, pro poenitente, epistolam ad S. Sedem mittere posset.

R. Negative ad primam partem; Affirmative ad secundam.

---

[20] S. C. S. Off., 16 Jun. 1897; Collect. II, 1971.
[21] S. C. S. Off., 9 Nov. 1898; Collect. II, 2023.
[22] S. C. S. Off., 5 Sept. 1900; Collect. II, 2095.

This entire matter is now contained in canon 2254 of the Code:

1. In casibus urgentioribus, si nempe censurae latae sententiae exterius servari nequeant sine periculo gravis scandali vel infamiae, aut si durum sit poenitenti in statu gravis peccati permanere per tempus necessarium ut Superior competens provideat, tunc quilibet confessarius in foro sacramentali ab eisdem, quoque modo reservatis, absolvere potest, iniuncto onere recurrendi, sub poena reincidentiae, intra mensem saltem per epistolam et per confessarium, si id fieri possit sine gravi incommodo, reticito nomine, ad S. Poenitentiariam vel ad Episcopum aliumve Superiorem praeditum facultate et standi eius mandatis.

2. Nihil impedit quominus poenitens, etiam post acceptam, ut supra, absolutionem, facto quoque recursu ad Superiorem, alium adeat confessarium facultate praeditum, ab eoque, repetita confessione saltem delicti cum censura, consequatur absolutionem; qua obtenta, mandata ab eodem accipiat, quin teneatur postea stare aliis mandatis ex parte Superioris supervenientibus.

3. Quod si in casu aliquo extraordinario hic recursus sit moraliter impossibilis, tunc ipsemet confessarius, excepto casu quo agatur de absolutione censurae de qua in can. 2367, potest absolutionem concedere sine onere de quo supra, iniunctis tamen de iure iniungendis, et imposita congrua poenitentia et satisfactione pro censura, ita ut poenitens, nisi intra congruum tempus a confessario praefiniendum poenitentiam egerit ac satisfactionem dederit, recidat in censuram.

In more urgent cases, therefore, that is when censures *latae sententiae* cannot be observed without danger of grave scandal or infamy or when it would be difficult for the penitent to remain in a state of mortal sin during the time necessary to go to a competent superior, any confessor can absolve from the censure in the sacramental forum, regardless of how the censure is reserved, but he must impose on the penitent, under penalty of reincidence, the obligation of recurring within a month to a competent superior.

This canon refers only to absolution from reserved censures; it does not refer to absolution from sins reserved *ratione sui.* This is clear from the word "censurae" in the canon itself and from the fact that the Code has already provided for the cessation of reservation of sins in urgent cases, in canon 900, No. 2. Consequently it is not correct to extend canon 2254 to reserved sins as some authors do.[23]

While canon 2254 refers only to reserved censures it embraces all censures *latae sententiae,* no matter how reserved, whether by common law, diocesan law, provincial or national law, or by the law of a Religious Superior. The canon makes no distinction and uses the general words "quoque modo reservatis." Again, therefore, authors are not justified in restricting it solely to Papal reservations.[24] The words "latae sententiae" specifically exclude censures reserved *ab homine* from the terms of this canon. The probable reason why they are not included is that they are public and consequently the person thus deprived of his reputation does not suffer grave injury by observing the censure.

The canon itself describes what is meant by an urgent case, namely if a censure cannot be observed externally without danger of grave scandal or infamy, or if it would be difficult for the penitent to remain in a state of mortal sin until faculties are obtained to absolve the censure. If, for example, a priest could not omit saying Mass without danger of grave scandal or loss of reputation, any confessor could absolve him from a reserved censure.

"Per tempus necessarium ut Superior competens provideat"—the competent superior referred to here does not merely mean the superior who inflicted the censure, but any competent superior who possesses the power to absolve such as the Apostolic Delegate, etc.[25]

Moral theologians teach that it may be a grave hardship for

---

[23] Arregui, No. 614.
[24] Noldin, III, 366.
[25] Vermeersch-Creusen, III, 454.

a penitent to remain in mortal sin longer than one day. There is question here of subjective hardship, that is the penitent must really feel it a hardship because, objectively, it is difficult for any one to remain in mortal sin longer than one day. The confessor should judge from the various circumstances, especially the dispositions of the penitent, whether or not it would be a hardship for the latter to remain in mortal sin during the time required to obtain the faculty to absolve from a competent superior. If the penitent lacks this strong desire to be absolved from sin as soon as possible, the confessor may and should strive to excite in him the strong desire of immediate absolution and if he succeeds he could then absolve him from the reserved censure.[26]

In an urgent case, any confessor can absolve from any censure *latae sententiae,* no matter how it is reserved. No censure is excepted, not even that inflicted for attempting to absolve an accomplice *in peccato turpi.* But the confessor can only absolve in the sacramental forum, and consequently the absolution is not valid for the external forum, unless it can be proven or legitimately presumed, though the one absolved can so act in the external forum provided no scandal is thereby caused.[27]

The absolution given in virtue of canon 2254 is direct.[28] The confessor who thus absolves in an urgent case is bound to impose upon the penitent the obligation of having recourse, within a month, to a competent superior and this obligation is to be imposed under penalty of reincidence. By failing to make the recourse, the penitent commits a new crime, serious disobedience of a grave ecclesiastical precept, and this new crime is punished by a censure of the same kind as that from which he was absolved. The censure of reincidence, though of precisely the same kind as the one absolved, is a com-

[26] Sabetti-Barrett, page 1022; Arregui, No. 617.

[27] Canon 2251.

[28] S. C. S. Off., 19 Aug. 1891, and 30 March 1892; Collect., II, 1764 and 1788.

pletely new censure, inflicted for a new crime and consequently it will not be incurred unless all the elements necessary for incurring censure are present in the new crime. From the wording of the Code, it appears that the censure of reincidence is *a iure* and not *ab homine.*[29] The return of the penitent to the confessor to receive the mandate of the superior is an essential part of the recursus as prescribed in § 1 of canon 2254 and so one who culpably failed to return would incur the new censure. Is the obligation of the confessor to impose the recursus so necessary that the absolution would be invalid if he failed to do so? This question does not refer to the case where it is morally impossible for the confessor to impose the obligation, referred to in the third part of this canon, but to the case where he should impose it. According to canon 11 only those laws are irritating in which it is either expressly or equivalently stated that the act is null; in the case in question it certainly is not expressly stated that "iniuncto onere recurrendi" is necessary for validity so the only question is whether or not the use of the ablative absolute is an equivalent statement of this. It is by no means certain that the use of the ablative absolute has this invalidating force; it is to be noted that no mention of it is made in canon 39. Consequently it seems at least probable that the obligation of imposing the recursus is only necessary for the liceity of the absolution.[30]

The recursus must be made "intra mensem." This period is to be measured from the time absolution was given and the obligation made known to the penitent. If, after promising to make the recursus, some cause arises to make it morally impossible for the penitent to return to the confessor within the designated time, he is not free from the obligation and is bound to return when the impediment ceases. The time designated is *tempus utile,* that is it does not run on if impeded and hence the penitent would not incur the censure of reincidence

[29] Cappello, page 34, note 4.
[30] Wernz, VI, 176, note 177; Lega, III, 150; D'Annibale, I, 351, note 5.

unless he failed to return within a period of thirty unimpeded days.

The recursus is to be made at least by letter and through a confessor. If there is any special difficulty connected with the sending of the letter by the confessor, if, for example, it might give rise to danger of violating the seal, the penitent himself could write the letter or go personally to the superior if this could be done without great difficulty. In most cases, however, the confessor must assume the duty of writing the letter.

The purpose of the recursus is to give the superior an opportunity of imposing a penance and of giving instruction and suggesting remedies to the penitent. Obviously, the object of the recursus is not to obtain absolution from the censure because the confessor has already directly absolved from it. The recursus is to be made to the Sacred Penitentiary or to a bishop or a superior who possesses the power to absolve from the reserved censure. If an Ordinary has the power, whether *a iure* or by special delegation, to absolve from the censure, the recourse may be made to him. It is not sufficient to make the recursus to a priest who has the faculty to absolve from the censure,[81] that is the penitent cannot make the recursus, as such, to a priest who possesses the power to absolve from the censure, but even though the penitent has already sent the letter to a competent superior, he can go to a confessor who possesses special power to absolve from the censure, and, having confessed the crime again, he can be absolved from the censure by this confessor and he is not then bound to carry out the mandate sent by the superior to whom he wrote.[82]

It is to be noted that the obligation of recursus is to be imposed when absolving from reserved censures—it is not to be imposed when absolving in virtue of canon 900 from sins reserved *ratione sui*. It will be explained later that the obligation of recursus is also to be imposed when a priest absolves

[81] S. C. S. Off., 19 Dec. 1900; Collect. II, 2098; Pont. Com. ad CC. auth. interpret., 12 Nov. 1922, AAS. XIV, 663.

[82] Canon 2254.

from reserved censures in danger of death but only when the censure absolved is *ab homine* or reserved *specialissimo modo* to the Holy See, whereas in urgent cases, it is to be imposed for all reserved censures, even for those reserved to or by the Ordinary.

Suppose that in some extraordinary case it is morally impossible to carry out the recursus, suppose, for example, that the penitent cannot write or go personally to the superior, and the confessor has to leave the place immediately and will never see the penitent again. In this case, the confessor can absolve without imposing the obligation of recourse. He should impose whatever obligations are otherwise to be imposed by law, that is the obligation of restitution or of avoiding the proximate occasion of sin or whatever else the case may demand; he should also impose a suitable penance and satisfaction for the censure and he should impose these under penalty of reincidence if the penitent fails to perform them within a suitable time determined by the confessor.[33] But there is one case in which, even though it is morally impossible to make the recursus, the confessor cannot absolve without imposing the obligation of making it and that is in the case of absolving from the censure incurred for attempting to absolve an accomplice *in peccato turpi*.[34]

C. Absolution From Reserved Censures in Danger of Death

The Church, anxious to provide every means possible for the eternal salvation of souls, is always most lenient to those who are in danger of death. For this reason she has always made special exceptions to her laws on reservations in the case of danger of death. The Council of Trent declared:[35] "Verumtamen pie admodum, ne hac ipsa occasione aliquis pereat, in eadem Ecclesia Dei costoditum fuit, ut nulla sit

---

[33] Canon 2254, §3; S. C. S. Off., 9 Nov. 1898; 7 Jun. 1899; 5 Sept. 1900; Collect. II, 2023, 2052, 2095.

[34] Canon 2367.

[35] Conc. Trident., sess. XIV, *De Poenitentia*, c. 7.

reservatio in articulo mortis, atque ideo, omnes sacerdotes quoslibet poenitentes a quibusvis peccatis et censuris absolvere possunt." This statement of Trent did not establish a new discipline, but merely declared a practise that existed previous to the Council.[36] However, when a delinquent, in danger of death, was absolved by a priest without the necessary power to absolve from reserved censures, the delinquent was bound, if he recuperated, to go to the superior and carry out his mandate—"si cessante postea periculo . . . se illi, a quo his cessantibus absolvi debeant, quam cito commode poterunt, contempserint praesentare mandatum ipsius super illis, pro quibus excommunicati fuerant humiliter recepturi, et satisfacturi prout iustitia suadebit, decernimus, ne sic censurae illudebant ecclesiasticae, in eamdem sententiam recidere ipso iure."[37] Before the Constitution *Apostolicae Sedis,* the obligation of going to the superior, in order to receive his mandate, bound all who became well after having been absolved, in danger of death, from a reserved censure, even though the censure was only reserved "simpliciter" to the Holy See. The Constitution *Apostolicae Sedis,* after enumerating the censures *latae sententiae,* reserved to the Holy See "speciali modo," continues: "Absolvere autem praesumentes sine debita facultate, etiam quovis praetextu excommunicationis vinculo Romano Pontifici reservatae innodotos se sciant, dummodo non sit agatur de mortis articulo, in quo tamen firma sit quoad absolutos obligatio standi mandatis Ecclesiae, si convaluerint."[38] By mentioning the obligation of receiving the mandate of the superior after the list of censures reserved "speciali modo," the Constitution implied that the obligation did not urge if the censure was reserved "simpliciter" to the Holy See. However, the point was not certain and as a consequence the following question was asked: "Utrum auctores moderni post Const. 'Apostolicae Sedis' (contra ius commune, cap. 'Eos qui,

[36] C. 14, C. XXVI, q.6; C.I, *De Privilegiis,* V, 7, *in Extravag.*
[37] c. 22, *De Sententia Excomm.,* V, II, in VI.
[38] Pius IX, const. *Apostolicae Sedis,* 12 Oct. 1869, No. 12; Collect. II, 1348.

22 De Sent. excomm. in VI, V. 11; cap. 'Ea noscitur,' 59, X, V. 39; et contra Rituale Romanum, 'De Poenit'; tit. III, c. i, n. 23) recte doceant, ei qui in articulo mortis a quolibet confessario a quibusvis censuris quomodocumque reservatis absolutus fuerit, tunc solummodo imponendam esse obligationem se sistendi Superiori recuperata valetudine, si agatur de absolutione a censuris 'speciali modo' Papae reservatis; an huismodi recursus ad Superiorem etiam necessarius sit in absolutione a censuris simpliciter Summo Pontifici reservatis?" The answer given by the Holy Office was: "Affirmative ad primam partem negative ad secundam partem, iuxta resolutionem fer. IV, 28 Iunii 1882."[39] This response made it certain that the obligation of recursus, when a censure was absolved in danger of death did not bind those who were absolved from a censure reserved "simpliciter" to the Holy See.

Because the Constitution "Apostolicae Sedis" made no mention of the penalty of reincidence if the delinquent failed to carry out the recursus, and because the phrase "standi mandatis Ecclesiae" used in the Constitution, did not clearly indicate the nature of the recursus, the following questions were asked: "1—An obligatio standi mandatis Ecclesiae a Bulla 'Apostolicae Sedis' imposita, sit sub poena reincidentiae vel non?" "2—An obligatio standi mandatis Ecclesiae in sensu Bullae 'Apostolicae Sedis,' idem sonat ac obligatio sistendi coram S. Pontifice, vel an ab illa debeat distingui?" The Holy Office answered: "Ad 1—Affirmative ad primam; negative ad secundam partem. Ad 2—Obligationem 'Standi mandatis Ecclesiae' importare onus sive per se, sive per confessarium, recurrendi ad S. Pontificem, eiusque mandatis obediendi, vel noram absolutionem petendi ab habente facultatem absolvendi a censuris S. Pontifici speciali modo reservatis."[40] Similar answers were given on January 13 and March 30, 1892.[41]

The law constituted by these various decrees and responses

---

[39] S. C. S. Off., 17 Jun. 1891, No. 3; Collect. II, 1756.
[40] S. C. S. Off., 19 Aug. 1891; Collect. II, 1764.
[41] Collect. II, 1777 ad 6 and 1788 ad 1, 2, 3, 4.

concerning absolution from reserved censures in danger of death was in effect to the promulgation of the Code and is substantially embodied in canons 882 and 2252.

The present law is that in danger of death all priests, even though not approved to hear confessions, can validly and licitly absolve any penitent from any sin or censure, regardless of how it is reserved or how notorious it may be, and this can be done even though a priest approved to hear confessions is at hand. The only exception to the latter clause is that a priest can not lawfully absolve his accomplice *in peccato turpi* even in danger of death if another priest can be had.[42]

The delinquent who is thus absolved, in danger of death, is bound, when freed from the danger, by the obligation of making a recursus to a competent superior if the censure from which he was absolved was *ab homine* or reserved *specialissimo modo* to the Holy See, and this obligation binds under penalty of reincidence. There are only two cases, therefore, in which the penitent, absolved in danger of death, is bound by the obligation of a recursus namely, if the censure is *ab homine,* or if it is reserved *specialissimo modo* to the Holy See. The obligation of the old law of making the recursus when the censure absolved in danger of death was reserved *speciali modo* no longer exists. If a penitent, in danger of death, is absolved by a simple priest from a censure reserved *speciali modo* or *simpliciter modo* to the Holy See, or reserved to or by the Ordinary, he is not bound to the recursus, unless the censure was *ab homine.* Hence, the obligation of recursus does not extend as far when absolution is given by a simple priest in danger of death, as it does when given in urgent cases—in urgent cases, outside of danger of death, the obligation must be imposed for all reserved censures.

If the censure was *ab homine,* the recursus is to be made to the Superior who inflicted the censure; if it was *latae sententiae* and reserved *specialissimo modo,* the recursus is to be made

[42] Canon 884.

either to the Sacred Penitentiary or to a Bishop or any other Superior who possesses the faculty to absolve from such censure.[43]

The recursus is to be made according to the norms of canon 2254, that is, within a month after the cessation of the danger or of recuperation, and at least by letter and through the confessor. A person may be considered to have recovered from the illness when he has reached that state of health in which he is able to perform the duty of the recursus without serious inconvenience. The danger of death need not necessarily arise from some intrinsic cause such as disease, serious wound, difficult child birth, extreme old age, etc.; it may also arise from some extrinsic cause such as a dangerous sea voyage, a state of war, etc.[44]

How far does the penalty of reincidence extend? Is the penitent bound merely to apply for and receive the mandate of the superior or is he also bound, under penalty of reincidence, to fulfill the mandate, that is, to perform the satisfaction and penance imposed? Vermeersch-Creusen express the opinion that this question was settled for the period previous to the Code by the response of March 30, 1892,[45] which stated: "obligationem standi mandatis Ecclesiae importare onus sive per se sive per confessarium ad S. Pontificem recurrandi eiusque mandatis obediendi, etc." While it is true, this defines the obligation of recursus it is not certain that it expressly extends the penalty of reincidence to failure to carry out the mandate of the Superior after accepting it. D'Annibale expressed the opinion that the penalty of reincidence did not extend to failure to carry out the mandate because when the penitent applied for and received the mandate there was no contumacy in merely failing to perform what the mandate enjoined.[46] The wording of canon 2252 seems to confirm this

[43] Canon 2252; Pont. Com. ad CC. auth. interpret., 12 Nov. 1922, AAS, XIV, 663.

[44] D'Annibale, *Com. in Const. Ap. Sedis,* 238; AAS. VII, 282.

[45] Collect. II, 1788; Vermeersch-Creusen, III, 452.

[46] D'Annibale, No. 354, note 20.

opinion. In this canon, the phrase "eorumque mandatis parendi" is placed after a semi-colon and thus completely separated from what precedes. As the canon is phrased and punctuated, there is certainly no grammatical connection between "sub poena reincidentiae" and "eorumque mandatis parendi." Consequently it seems that the penalty of reincidence is not to be extended to failure to carry out the mandate .after receiving it.[47]

[47] Arregui, No. 617; Noldin, III, 367.

BIBLIOGRAPHY

Acta Apostolicae Sedis, Romae 1909–.

Acta Sanctae Sedis, 41 vol., Romae 1865–1908.

ARREGUI, ANTONIUS, S. J., *Summarium Theologiae Moralis,* 5 ed., Romae 1920.

AYRINHAC, H. A., S. S., *Penal Legislation in the New Code of Canon Law,* New York, 1920.

BENEDICTUS XIV, *De Synodo Diocesana,* Romae 1806.

BLAT, ALBERTUS, O. P., *Commentarium Textus Codicis Iuris Canonici, Liber* III, Romae 1919.

Canoniste Contemporain, Le, vol. 43, Paris 1920.

CAPPELLO, FELIX M., S. J., *De Censuris iuxta Codicem Iuris Canonici,* Augustae Taurinorum 1919.

Catholic Encyclopedia, vol. III, article *Censures,* New York, 1907–1912.

CAVIGIOLI, IOANNES, *De Censuris latae sententiae quae in Codice Iuris Canonici continentur,* Torino 1918.

CERATO, PROSODOCIMUS, *Censurae vigentes ipso facto a Codice Iuris Canonici excerptae,* Patavii 1918.

CHARLES AUGUSTINE, Rev. P., O. S. B., *A Commentary on the New Code of Canon Law,* St. Louis 1918.

CHELODI, IOANNES, *Jus Poenale,* Tridenti 1920.

Codex Iuris Canonici Pii X Pontificis Maximi iussu digestus Benedicti Papae XV auctoritate promulgatus, Romae 1917.

Codicis Iuris Canonici Fontes, Cura Emi Petri Card. Gasparri Editi vol. I, Romae 1923.

Collectanea Sacrae Congregationis de Propaganda Fide, 2 vol., Romae 1907.

CONCINA, F. DANIELE, O. P., *Theologia Christiana,* Neapoli 1775.

Corpus Iuris Canonici, 2 vol., Lipsae 1922.

D'ANNIBALE, JOSEPHUS, *In Constitutionem "Apostolicae Sedis" qua Censurae latae sententiae limitantur Commentarii,* 4 ed., Prati 1894.

D'ANNIBALE, JOSEPHUS, *Summa Theologiae Moralis, pars* I, ed. 3a., Romae 1897.

DE LUGO, IOANNES, S. J., *Disputationes Scholasticae et Morales,* vol. V, Parisiis 1868.

DIANA, ANTONII, *Opera Omnia,* vol. I, Venetiis 1728.

FANFANI, LUDOVICUS, O. P., *De Iure Religiosorum,* Taurinorum 1920.

FARRUGIA, P. NICHOLAUS, Ord. S. Aug., *De Casuum Conscientiae Reservatione,* ed 2, Augustae Taurinorum 1922.

FERRERES, IOANNES, S. J., *Compendium Theologiae Moralis,* vol. 2, ed. 9, Barcinone 1918–1919.

GENICOT-SALSMANS, *Institutiones Theologiae Moralis, ed. 3, post Codicem,* Bruxellis 1922.

GURY-BALLERINI, *Compendium Theologiae Moralis,* ed. 9, Romae 1887.

HARDOUIN, *Acta Conciliorum,* 2 vol., Paris 1715.

HINSCHIUS, PAUL, *System des Katholischen Kirchenrechts,* vol. 4, Berlin 1888.

Irish Ecclesiastical Record, vol. XVIII.

Irish Theological Quarterly, vol. XII.

LAYMANN, PAULO, S. J., *Theologia Moralis,* Patavii 1732.

LEGA, MICHAEL, *Praelectiones in Textum Iuris Canonici,* vol. 3, Romae 1899.

LEHMKUHL, AUGUSTINUS, S. J., *Theologia Moralis,* ed. 11a., Friburgi Brisgoviae 1910.

MANSI, J. D., *Sacrorum Conciliorum Nova et Amplissima Collectio,* 31 vols., Venetiis 1759–1798.

MINGE, *Patrologia Latina.*

NOLDIN, H., S. J., *De Poenis Ecclesiasticis,* Oeniponte 1921.

NOLDIN, H., S. J., *Summa Theologiae Moralis,* vol. III, ed. 13, Oeniponte 1920.

PIGHI, J. B., *Censurae et Irregularitates,* ed 5, Veronae 1919.

PRÜMMER, DOMINICUS M., O. P., *Manuale Theologiae Moralis,* Friburgi Brisgoviae 1923.

SABETTI-BARRETT, *Compendium Theologiae Moralis,* ed. 28, New York 1919.

S. ALPHONSUS, *Theologia Moralis,* Torino 1887.

SANCHEZ, THOMA, S. J., *Disputationes de Sancto Matrimonii Sacramenta,* Antverpiae 1626.

SOLE, JACOBUS, *De Delictis et Poenis,* Romae 1920.

SUAREZ, FRANCISCUS, S. J., *Opera Omnia,* vol. 22, Parisiis 1866.

TANQUEREY, A., *Synopsis Theologiae Moralis,* ed. 5, Romae 1919.

THOMASSIN, LUDOVICO, *Vetus et Nova Ecclesiae Disciplina,* Mogontiaci 1787.

VAN ESPEN, ZEGERI BERNARDI, *Opera Omnia Canonica, pars* II *tit. VI,* Lovanii 1732.

VERMEERSCH-CREUSEN, *Epitome Iuris Canonici,* Mechlinae 1921.

WATKINS, O. D., *A History of Penance,* 2 vols., London 1920.

WERNZ, FRANCISCUS, S. J., *Ius Decretalium,* vol. VI, Prati 1914.

Universitas Catholica Americae

Washingtonii, D. C.

Facultas Iuris Canonici

1923–1924

No. 20

DEUS LUX MEA

THESES

QUAS

AD DOCTORATUS GRADUM

IN

IURE CANONICO

APUD UNIVERSITATEM CATHOLICAM AMERICAE

CONSEQUENDUM

PUBLICE PROPUGNABIT

EDUARDUS VINCENTIUS DARGIN

SACERDOS ARCHIDIOECESIS NEO EBORACENSIS

IURIS CANONICI LICENTIATUS

HORA IX A. M. DIE XXVI MAII A. D. MCMXXIV

I. Canones 1–7. De Ambitu Codicis Iuris Canonici.
II. Canones 12–14. De Subiecto Legis Ecclesiasticae.
III. Canones 25–30. De Consuetudine.
IV. Canones 36–37. De Subiecto Rescriptorum.
V. Canones 80–86. De Dispensationibus.
VI. Canones 91–95. De Domicilio et Quasi-domicilio.
VII. Canones 111–117. De Clericorum Adscriptione alicui dioecesi.
VIII. Canones 196–210. De Potestate Ordinaria et Delegata.
IX. Canones 520–527. De Confessariis Religiosarum.
X. Canones 727–730. De Simonia.
XI. Canones 738–744. De Ministro Baptismi.
XII. Canones 750–751. De Baptismo Infantium Acatholicorum.
XIII. Canones 762–769. De Patrinis.
XIV. Canones 873–875. De Iurisdictione ad Confessiones excipiendas.
XV. Canon 882. De Absolutione in periculo mortis.
XVI. Canon 883. De Iurisdictione Sacerdotis Iter Arripientis.
XVII. Canon 893. De Reservatione Peccatorum.
XVIII. Canones 893, 2246, 2247. De Distinctione inter Reservationem Peccatorum et Censurarum.
XIX. Canones 895–896. Quomodo Reservato Iure Utendum.
XX. Canones 897–898. Quot Casus Reservandi et quinam?
XXI. Canon 900. Quomodo Reservatio vi careat ipso iure.
XXII. De Effectu Ignorantiae Reservationis.
XXIII. Canones 881, 883, 900. An Subditus alterius Diocesis ligatus Reservatione Episcopali.
XXIV. Canones 1043–1044. De Dispensationibus Matrimonialibus urgente periculo mortis.
XXV. Canones 1060–1064. De Matrimoniis Mixtis.
XXVI. Canones 1070–1071. De Impedimento Disparitatis Cultus.
XXVII. Canon 1072. De Impedimento Ordinis.
XXVIII. Canones 1120–1127. De Privilegio Paulino.
XXIX. Canones 1553–1554. De Competentia Ecclesiae in Iudiciis.
XXX. Canones 1556–1558. De Causis Majoribus.
XXXI. Canon 1560. De Foro Necessario.
XXXII. Canones 1561–1568. De Foris Voluntariis.
XXXIII. Canones 1580–1584. De Auditoribus et Relatoribus.
XXXIV. Canones 1586–1590. De Promotore Iustitiae et Defensore Vinculi.
XXXV. Canones 1594–1596. De Tribunali Secundae Instantiae.
XXXVI. Canones 1636–1639. De Loco et Tempore Iudicii.
XXXVII. Canones 1701–1705. De Exstinctione Actionum.
XXXVIII. Canones 1756–1757. De eis qui Testes esse possunt.
XXXIX. Canon 2229. De eis qua a poenis latae sententiae excusant.

XL. Canon 2254. De Absolutione a censura reservata in casibus urgentioribus.

Ius Publicum.

XLI. De Erroribus quoad Formam Regiminis Ecclesiae.
XLII. De Potestate Coactiva Ecclesiae.
XLIII. De Electione Romanis Pontificis.
XLIV. De Iure Gladii.
XLV. De Relatione Concilli Oecuminici ad Romanum Pontificem.
XLVI. De Iure Censurandi Libros.
XLVII. De Ratione Metropolitanatus.
XLVIII. De Divina Institutione Episcopatus.
XLIX. De Iure Civili quoad Matrimonium.
L. De Concordatis In Genere.

International Law.

LI. Nature of International Law.
LII. Fundamental Principles of International Law.
LIII. Sources of International Law.
LIV. General Rights and Obligations of States.
LV. Diplomatic Agents.
LVI. Piracy.
LVII. Jurisdiction over Vessels.
LVIII. The Monroe Doctrine.
LIX. Extradition.
LX. Consuls.

Vidit Sacra Facultas:

PHILIPPUS BERNARDINI, S.T.D., J.U.D., Decanus.
H. LUDOVICUS MOTRY, S.T.D., J.C.D., p.t.a Secretis.

Vidit Rector Universitatis:

THOMAS J. SHAHAN, S.T.D., J.U.L.

www.ingramcontent.com/pod-product-compliance
Lightning Source LLC
LaVergne TN
LVHW050159080826
844660LV00012B/316

* 9 7 8 0 8 1 3 2 2 2 1 1 0 *